Praise for
Unlocking Parental Intelligence

"Dr. Laurie Hollman's book, *Unlocking Parental Intelligence*, has accomplished a notable feat in describing sophisticated theories of child development and behavior and offering a window into the inner workings of the minds of parents and children while managing to make these ideas clear and easily accessible to parents. The book is clearly and beautifully written and Dr. Hollman conveys throughout a non-judgmental, non-critical stance where the reader feels her genuine empathy for the parent and child and their struggles. Her empathy transforms the parents into becoming more empathic with their children.

What distinguishes her guide from other parenting books is her emphasis on the important need 'to understand' the meaning behind the misbehavior of the child or adolescent, rather than assuming to know what the misbehavior means and reacting in the moment. She offers stories about eight children and their parents and takes you along on each of the journeys, while describing the parents' gradual awakening that leads to insight about their child and also to greater self-knowledge. Of special note is Dr. Hollman's ability to enable parents to look deeply into their own minds and to understand how their past generational histories are carried over into their feelings and dealings with their own children. This is a very admirable parenting book.

I strongly recommend this book to mental health professionals and educators working with children and adolescents, who could also use it as a text book for child therapists."

—PHYLLIS BEREN, PhD, Co-Director, Institute for
Psychoanalytic Training and Research Child and Adolescent
Psychotherapy Program, NY, NY; Training and Supervising
Analyst at the Institute for Psychoanalytic Training and
Research and the Contemporary Freudian Society

"An unwavering parent-child connection is the most protective force in our kids' lives. It is critical to whether they will be resilient today and poised to thrive tomorrow. Reacting impulsively to our children's actions can interfere with our ability to make wise decisions, and even damage the stability of our connections. Dr. Hollman's practical model offers us a framework to easily access the innate Parental Intelligence that allows us to feel fully and think and respond effectively. Her detailed examples masterfully make these strategies our own as we learn to better understand our children. This book will undoubtedly foster the kind of connections that will position us to better prepare our children to navigate their lives safely and successfully."

—KENNETH R. GINSBURG, MD, MS Ed., Professor of Pediatrics, Division of Adolescent Medicine, The Children's Hospital of Philadelphia and the University of Pennsylvania School of Medicine; Author, *Building Resilience in Children and Teens* and *Raising Kids to Thrive*

"With candor and compassion, Laurie Hollman, PhD, teaches parents about Parental Intelligence. In her groundbreaking book, she draws on contemporary child development theory offering parents an easy-to-follow, five-step program for conflict resolution. Parents will learn how to understand the underlying determinants to their child's behavior, how to "read" non-verbal as well as verbal communication, and how to create an open dialogue. As an experienced child and family therapist, Dr. Hollman is in a unique position to talk to parents. She provides fictionalized accounts of real problems. Dr. Hollman teaches parents how to understand their own expectations, listen to their child's communication, and take into account the meaning behind the child's behavior and how it relates to their developmental level. Along the way, parents will build a stronger, healthier bond with their child. Just as Dr. Hollman teaches parents to interact more effectively and empathically with their children, she writes with empathy and understanding as she teaches parents this proven and user-friendly method of parenting. Dr. Hollman's book is an essential guide for every parent."

—RENA GREENBLATT, PhD, Psychoanalyst; Child and Adolescent Clinical Psychologist; Learning Disabilities and ADHD Specialist; Faculty, New York University

"Dr. Laurie Hollman's informative and highly engaging new book, taps into resources parents possess and provides a useful approach to creating the kind of parent-child relationship that promotes child development and parenting satisfaction. Dr. Hollman illustrates through vivid examples, with which all parents will be able to identify, how emotional triggers can sabotage empathy and she demonstrates how her Five Steps to 'unlocking Parental Intelligence' lead to problem solving. It is essential reading for all parents and professionals who seek a greater understanding of children's behavior and their own reactions to it."

—ILENE SACKLER LEFCOURT, Director, Sackler Lefcourt Center for Child Development, NY, NY; Faculty, Columbia University Center for Psychoanalytic Training and Research Parent-Infant Program

"Children, no matter how old they are, often express with their troubled behaviors a wish to communicate. The challenge is to decipher their message. Laurie Hollman, PhD, shows us with talent, how one may think about a family history in a transgenerational mode and resituate the child's departure from their usual ways in this context. Guided this way, parents can adjust their focus to the needs of their children and find their way out of devastating impasses. By using a precise description of blocked family situations, she shows us how to take consideration of unconscious transmission in parental situations and slowly unknot conflicts. With this book, Dr. Hollman provides a precious accompaniment for families."

—MYRIAM SZEJER, MD, Child psychiatrist, psychoanalyst, Montrouge, France; Faculty, of Medicine, University of Versailles-Saint Quentin en Yvelines; author, *Talking to Babies: Healing with Words on a Maternity Ward*

"Dr. Laurie Hollman's book has been extremely clarifying and helpful to me, not only as a parent and step-parent, but also as a psychologist in my clinical work with families. Dr. Hollman possesses an exceptional gift in providing parents with the confidence to unlock the door to the tools they already possess to enhance their understanding and enjoyment of one of life's greatest gifts—their children—thereby enabling parents, through self-reflection, empathy, and wisdom, to cultivate their children's optimal development within a loving and secure family framework. This book is also very helpful to parents whose children have pervasive developmental disorders and other special needs.

Dr. Hollman also gives us promise for future generations of children raised with Parental Intelligence who grow up and want to be leaders. Learning the skills of Parental Intelligence is a source for instilling creative interpersonal, problem solving, and leadership abilities essential to fulfilling, productive lives in the next generation who will lead us in many local, national, and global arenas."

—LYNN SESKIN, PsyD, School and Clinical Psychologist, Specialty in the Treatment of Children and Adolescents with Pervasive Developmental Disorders

"It is my pleasure as Editor of *Moms Magazine,* a community of parenting experts and moms sharing real-life experiences of parenthood, to say that Laurie Hollman, PhD, is one of our go-to experts because she provides a clear approach to guide moms on their parenthood journey through her Parental Intelligence model.

We live in a fast-paced world and never before have we seen such a shift in the way we live our lives with social media, the 24-hour news cycle and emerging technologies—and this all applies to parenting, too. There is so much information out there—and so many opinions. We need an expert voice, like Dr. Laurie Hollman's, who can help break through the clutter and give us easy-to-follow advice that tells us what to think about as we parent. This is what our readers want, and it is presented in *Unlocking Parental Intelligence: Finding Meaning in Your Child's Behavior.*"

—JUDY I. COHEN, Managing Editor, *Moms Magazine*

"Theory of mind—that is, understanding people as mental beings—is a key topic in Developmental Psychology research. And Parental Intelligence is theory of mind in action! Dr. Hollman's excellent book shows how you can be aware of your own thoughts and feelings while also keeping in mind your child's different thoughts and feelings. This mindset can help solve behavior problems without using punishment."

—JANET WILDE ASTINGTON, PhD, Professor Emerita, Institute of Child Study, Department of Human Development and Applied Psychology, University of Toronto; editor, *Minds in the Making*

"So often, families are stuck. Concerned and caring parents feel that they have tried everything and just don't know what to do. In this very helpful book, psychoanalyst Laurie Hollman, PhD, wisely encourages us to take a step back. Dr. Hollman teaches parents to ask why, to listen with greater empathy, and look for the meaning in their children's behavior. She shows that when we do this, we will have better relationships with our children and help them find better solutions to the problems in their lives."

—KENNETH BARISH, PhD, Clinical Associate Professor of Psychology, Weill Medical College, Cornell University; author of *Pride and Joy: A Guide to Understanding Your Child's Emotions and Solving Family Problems*

"Dr. Laurie Hollman's book, *Unlocking Parental Intelligence,* is a clear and concise guide to parenting. Learning to understand the meaning of a child's behavior and dealing with it in an empathic, problem-solving way is an effective approach to raising children who are self-confident and able to eventually understand and control their own behaviors. This is a guide to thoughtful parenting that is dynamic and aids both the parent and the child in feeling able to adjust to changing issues as the child goes through different developmental stages. It is a book I will recommend to my patients and the techniques are helpful to teach to therapists who work with issues related to parenting."

—MARIE OPPEDISANO, PhD, Psychoanalyst; Child and Adolescent Clinical Psychologist; served as researcher, Long Island Jewish-Hillside Medical Center, New Hyde Park, NY

"As well as being highly rewarding being a parent can also be challenging. Dr. Laurie Hollman's book provides an approach through which parents can resolve difficulties with their children by understanding their children's actions as well as reflecting on their own reactions. She illustrates her approach with many insightful examples of working out difficulties with children in ways that should result in parents enjoying their children even more."

—JEREMY CARPENDALE, PhD, Professor, Developmental Psychology, Simon Fraser University, Burnaby, British Columbia; author, *How Children Develop Social Understanding*

"This enlightening book offers a clear, practical approach to parenting that promotes relationships between parent and child. Dr. Hollman presents insightful parenting skills by sharing real-to-life family histories, experiences, and solutions. Parents are encouraged to learn from their own past histories, given permission to have made mistakes in how they handled situations with their child, and shown how to move to a more positive understanding and resolution of the current 'crisis.' The families we get to know have children of different ages, different marital situations, and different challenges that make their families unique, yet familiar. Through use of the steps taught in the book parents are led to realize that the 'offense' is not always the behavior that must be adjusted. The plan encourages communication between parent and child which will lead to smoother resolution of future issues. What I like best about this beautifully well-written approach is that it will facilitate a calmer environment in the home and family with more productive dialogue between the parents and between parent and child."

—DOTTIE DEL GAUDIO, MSEd, Director and Teacher,
UMC Nursery School, Huntington-Cold Spring Harbor, NY

Unlocking Parental Intelligence

Published by Familius LLC, www.familius.com

Familius books are available at special discounts for bulk purchases for sales promotions
or for family or corporate use. Special editions, including personalized covers, excerpts of
existing books, or books with corporate logos, can be created in large quantities for special
needs. For more information, contact Premium Sales at 559-876-2170 or email
specialmarkets@familius.com.

Library of Congress Catalog-in-Publication Data
2015940077

Print ISBN 9781942934042
Ebook ISBN 9781942934530
Hardcover ISBN 9781942934547

Printed in the United States of America

Edited by Brooke Jorden
Cover design by David Miles
Book design by Brooke Jorden

10 9 8 7 6 5 4 3 2 1

First Edition

Unlocking Parental Intelligence

FINDING MEANING IN YOUR CHILD'S BEHAVIOR

WITH A SELECTION OF STORIES ABOUT MOTHERS AND FATHERS
WHO DISCOVER WISDOM IN A NEW PARENTING MINDSET

LAURIE HOLLMAN, PH.D.

To Jeff, for his patience, compassion, and love as a husband and father.

Acknowledgments

I am grateful to all those who have inspired and helped me with this book. I must begin with my husband, Jeff, my partner in life, whose talented writing and editorial skills, along with his empathy for children, have always strengthened my resolve to put my ideas into words. He faithfully read every word more than once, discussing my concepts as they were formulated, as well as editing them once I put them into written language. Both his facility with language and psychological understanding supported the evolution of this book. He seemed to get to know the characters in my stories and feel, along with me, their struggles and accomplishments.

My gratitude also goes to my oldest son, David, who was raised with Parental Intelligence. I watch David as a father carry out his style of Parental Intelligence with his wife, Claire, my lovely daughter-in-law who feels like my daughter. Both discussed parenting with me, clarifying my ideas. David's eloquent use of language helped me find words to express my thoughts that deepened my capacity to convey my ideas clearly and succinctly. Observing David and Claire's empathy with their sons gives me lasting joy.

My appreciation extends to my younger son, Rich, whose words grace the last chapter of the book. His humanistic outlook on how people relate to each other was encouraging as I wrote. He helped me clarify the focus of part three of the book: "The Future with Parental Intelligence." He, too, of course was raised with Parental Intelligence and honors all those around him with his capacity for discerning others' emotions and responding intelligently and empathically.

I give thanks to Helga Schier, PhD, my editor prior to beginning the publishing process. Along with Jeff, she read every word, shared insights about writing, and gave me the security of knowing an excellent, experienced developmental editor was by my side.

With pleasure, I thank Marcelle Soviero for her encouragement of my writing and her belief in the premises of this book that led her to write the well thought out, enthusiastic foreword that opens this book.

I would also like to thank Judy I. Cohen, Managing Editor of *Moms Magazine*. By giving me a special column titled "Parental Intelligence," she has given me the opportunity to write articles about my concepts and reach a multitude of parents due to the very broad circulation of her magazine.

I am grateful to the industrious, delightful staff at Familius Press, including Christopher Robbins for always being available even while carrying out his executive role, Erika Riggs for her wonderful guidance, and David Miles for his artistry and design talents.

I also want to give thanks to Brooke Jorden, my gifted editor at Familius. In her easygoing, collaborative way, we refined my book and brought it to fruition. She warmly offered editorial insight and honed my language and thinking. Her careful attention to detail and responsiveness to all my inquiries was just what I needed.

In addition, I thank the great many parents and their children in my practice over the years who inspired my desire to write this book so others could benefit from their accomplishments in building strong, growing lives. With their courage to learn new ways of understanding themselves and finding meaning in their relationships that built family ties, I was encouraged to integrate what I had learned and incorporate it in this book for others.

As my psychoanalytic training and research has progressed throughout the many years of my practice, I have incorporated the voices of so many others who have influenced me and broadened and deepened the dimensions of my psychological horizons.

I can't conclude without thanking the future generation: my loving grandsons Zander, age seven, and Eddie, age four. Hearing their remarkable use of language at such young ages and watching their vibrant youthfulness always inspired me to keep on writing. When they confide in me their personal thoughts and wishes, I am reminded of the essence of Parental Intelligence: the close bonds it brings between parent and child, grandparent and grandchild.

Contents

Foreword

During the time when I started reading *Unlocking Parental Intelligence,*
my thirteen-year-old son began shutting himself in his room, and if/
when he came out, he never let go of his grip on his phone. Family din-
ners were tense, as we had to coax him out of his bedroom and insist on
"no phone at the table." This went on for months, and all the while, I told
myself he was "just being a teen." But I knew it was more than that. I felt
pressured; I could not sleep. In the wee hours, I asked myself as I had a
thousand times before, *Why was my son doing these things?*

Then I read *Unlocking Parental Intelligence,* in which Dr. Hollman
writes, "all parents wonder why their children do the things they do."
Aha! I was not alone. But more than that, Dr. Hollman, with kindness
and candor, explained *what I could do* to find out the answer to that
question. She had an actionable, five-step plan that would facilitate conversation with my son.

I put Dr. Hollman's plan into practice. I self-reflected, and I searched
for the meaning behind my son's behavior. I considered his verbal and
nonverbal clues and took into account my own motivations. Using this
book as a blueprint, I developed a way in which to be more empathic
with my son. And then I spoke to him.

My assumptions about his underlying behavior were correct—something else was wrong; there was a bigger reason why he was closing
himself off in his room and texting tirelessly. Unbeknownst to me, he
had been asked out by a girl, had failed a math test, and was worried
about his forthcoming cello recital and travel baseball tryouts. (Since he
was a dedicated math student, cellist, and baseball player, I hadn't antic-
ipated his anxiety, nor had I any idea there might be a girl in the picture

since my older son did not date until he was sixteen). As a result of our discussions, I stopped doubting my intuition and instead was lifted and empowered by Dr. Hollman's rhetorical question: Who else knows a child as well as a parent does?

My son and I benefited from Dr. Hollman's intelligent approach—from her patience (you can do the steps in any order; you can go back and try again) and her perspective (one of open-mindedness). In the end, our relationship has improved, and we have a new way to communicate.

Written in a clear narrative format, Dr. Hollman explains the power of understanding ourselves and our pasts in order to understand our assumptions, our reactions, and most of all, our children. As I read the compelling personal stories gleaned from her thirty years as a psychoanalyst and psychotherapist, I fell into a place where I had never been as a parent—a place where I saw the challenges I was having with my son as an opportunity, a moment of ripe possibility to grow closer to my son. This transformation was a clarification as well as a source of joy—and relief.

As an editor of a magazine for mothers, I have read hundreds of articles and dozens of books about parenting. As my own five children have grown, I have amassed a huge collection of such books; many have great advice, but *Unlocking Parental Intelligence* combines research, experience, and case studies into actionable steps that will make a difference for the conscientious parent. Further, parents who use Parental Intelligence will affect future generations of children who become parents. The five steps of Parental Intelligence become a way of life for families. Parental Intelligence gives children who want to be leaders the foundation they need to relate to a broad spectrum of people around the world because they have a grounding in relating and communicating with others that began early in their upbringing and is now a part of who they are. No other parenting book offers such wisdom for so many generations to come.

With this wonderful book, after eighteen years of mothering, I learned to trust my instincts, find meaning in my son's behavior, and, perhaps most importantly, better understand my own actions, principles, and parenting philosophy. Additionally, my son now has the opportunity, when he becomes an adult and even a parent, to continue to carry out the philosophy of Parental Intelligence by knowing how to look for meaning behind people's actions and by finding ways to communicate effectively with his own voice.

Marcelle Soviero
Editor-in-Chief
Brain, Child: The Magazine for Thinking Parents

Introduction

Do you ever wonder *why* your child behaves the way she does? How many times in a single day do you ask yourself, "Why did she do that?" Even little things can throw you. Your three-year-old lies about brushing his teeth. He lied? At age *three*? Sometimes it's subtle. For example, your teenage daughter tells you about her day, something she rarely does. Why now? Is she just feeling chatty or did something happen that she's not quite ready to tell you yet? Sitting in a parent-teacher conference, or even a principal's office, you may ask yourself, "Why did my child behave that way? How am I supposed to handle this?"

We've all experienced that awful feeling of fear, surprise, or incomprehension when our kids do something unusual, unimaginable, or outright distressing. And when nothing changes, despite our best efforts to address the behavior, all we can do is wonder, "Why?"

It's common to have moments of despair, when you feel that parenting is beyond you; when you believe that the job requires a special kind of intelligence that wasn't encrypted on your brain and you're waiting for the time when you can sustain—for just one day—that important parent-child bond psychologists say is necessary for a healthy family life.

In this book, I am going to give you a new perspective on behaviors that may confound you and cause you powerful inner pressure or even panic. I'm going to lead you up a path that enlightens, uplifts, and relieves you as you learn how to unmask the meanings behind your child's behavior. As you continue to practice this process, you will become a *meaning-maker*, empowered to read your child's actions like an open book. Using the tools I provide, I will help you experience the heightened energy and deep satisfaction that come with unlocking your Parental Intelligence.

Parenting offers many humorous, precious situations—like the time you invited fifty people to your daughter's first birthday party and she pressed her chubby fingers into the center of the chocolate cake you baked, swirled them around, and then happily put them into your mouth like there was no distance between the two of you. If only it could stay that way; if only that instant could last forever, like a memento that reminds you of the cow that jumped over the moon. You hoped she could have a dreamy childhood and never stop believing that family life is all chocolate cake. We all wish it could stay simple—all good humor and pure joy.

But parenting can have a difficult side, too—like the time your eight-year-old fled the house yelling, "I'm running away! Why do you ruin everything? You never get it." He came back, exhausted after fifteen tortuous minutes speeding around the front yard like a freight train that had gone off its track and landed in a deep ditch. You stood by the window, watching him, heart pounding, worried and scared. You felt winded, as if *you* were the locomotive spinning off the track. Tears pushed out from your tired eyes. And your son came in defeated and spent. Even though he returned, you knew there was some deeper meaning behind what he did. But what do you do when you're afraid that whatever is wrong will shadow you and your child everywhere? The stakes are high.

I've been inspired to write this book after three decades of clinical work as a psychoanalyst, working with both mothers and fathers who came to me at different stages in their parenting careers, questioning what to do to salvage their parent-child relationships, asking how to put their children back on a reasonable course, and wondering how to find meaning in their family lives. I am grateful to those parents for telling me how unlocking their Parental Intelligence has benefited their families.

The circumstances and backgrounds of these mothers and fathers vary greatly—they had children of different ages, they were at different stages of their parenting lives, and they came from different economic and social backgrounds. Yet, I discovered that they had some crucial things in common. They were conscientious, thinking parents. And most importantly, they all wanted to understand their kids. This was key.

They were all searching for that special intelligence needed for respectful parenting, even if they didn't quite know how to ask for it. What they were searching for is what I call *Parental Intelligence*. I coined this term because I believe parenting requires the persistence and rigor of an intelligence that can be honed with the right tools and life experience.

I believe parents should never be underestimated—even when they doubt themselves. With a clearly designed pathway, you can unlock your Parental Intelligence, access and harness your parenting capacities, and solve the most important problems your children are facing.

With Parental Intelligence, you will figure out the *whys* behind your child's behavior. Knowing why your child behaves a certain way will allow you to find the best approach to dealing with the behavior. Understanding why your child acts out, disobeys, or behaves in disruptive and disturbing ways is the key to preventing the recurrence of the behavior. Parental Intelligence provides that understanding.

I have narrowed down and systemized the learning process into five steps that will unlock your Parental Intelligence. And I will illustrate—through examples of many difficult scenarios of compelling family situations—how to use these positive parenting steps in order to achieve the outcomes you desire.

These five steps reveal how behavior mirrors the workings of your child's mind. With Parental Intelligence, you enter the inner world of your child and understand where he or she is coming from. You will no longer focus initially on stopping misbehavior, but you will first try to understand the meaning behind the misbehavior, and even consider it a useful communication. This approach not only prevents undesired behavior more effectively, it also strengthens parent-child relationships. You and your child grow together.

Three basic interrelated tenets lie behind Parental Intelligence: (1) behaviors have underlying meanings; (2) once parents understand how their own minds are working, they are liberated to understand their child—how their child's mind is working; (3) once meanings are clear, options surface by which to change unwanted behaviors. When these

three core concepts come into play, the ambiance of family life fundamentally changes.

When parents get to know themselves—their reactions to their child
and the many influences on their parenting—they find that they gain a
better understanding of their child who wants to be known as he or she
actually is. This means that parents no longer focus on the child's specific
misbehavior as the overarching troubles and problems emerge. When
those problems are addressed, the original misbehavior loses importance
and usually stops.

The book is divided into three parts. "Part One: Developing Your
Parental Intelligence" describes the theory behind Parental Intelligence
and the five steps toward creating it: *Stepping Back, Self-Reflecting,
Understanding Your Child's Mind, Understanding Your Child's
Development,* and *Problem Solving.* The five steps are geared to both
women and men who become parents and look to support their children's growth, development, and happiness. In today's society, there is a
broad array of roles that mothers and fathers take on as they participate
in parenting. These varied roles are readily adapted to family life as parents use their Parental Intelligence.

"Part Two: Stories of Parental Intelligence in Practice" offers eight
short stories about parents using Parental Intelligence with their children. Each family portrait reveals that as parents understand themselves,
they can better understand their children. With these understandings,
misbehaviors become a catalyst to change. As open dialogue evolves,
parents discover and clarify the meanings behind the behaviors. In turn,
parents and children grapple with the underlying struggles that, though
not apparent at first, were hidden behind the behaviors. Once brought to
light, problems can be solved.

These stories about infants, children, and adolescents—including
three with special needs: ADHD, a pervasive developmental disorder,
and depression—demonstrate the broad spectrum to which the five steps
of Parental Intelligence apply. The eight stories focus on the pivotal roles

fathers and mothers can have in their child's behavior and development.

I have written fictionalized accounts of real behaviors and family dynamics to preserve the privacy of my patients and people I've come across in daily life, but the problems and their resolutions are noteworthy and considerable.

"Part Three: The Future with Parental Intelligence" describes a world where Parental Intelligence has become commonplace. This philosophy of parenting has ramifications at familial and societal levels. I discuss how this parenting approach provides a meeting ground where parents and children get to know each other in profound ways as they solve present problems that affect their future values and directions. Children of such families will have the skills to work through conflicts in their daily lives, work lives, and future relationships.

This book doesn't have an ending. Many mothers and fathers raising their children with Parental Intelligence have told me that using these principles as a guide have led to a new way of being together—a new parenting life. And for myself, I learned the most about raising children by becoming a parent to my two outstanding, spirited sons, David and Rich. They continue to give me the privilege of carrying out my most important job—being a mother. I humbly know that Parental Intelligence helps you feel love in ways you never dreamed possible. Parental Intelligence provides a vision of hope: a pathway for parents to better understand both themselves and their children at all ages and developmental levels. Using Parental Intelligence, parents support their children as they solve their problems and lead loving, satisfying lives.

PART ONE

DEVELOPING YOUR
PARENTAL INTELLIGENCE

Chapter One

The New Parenting Mindset

*The voices of empathic parents become the
inner voices of self-assured, secure children.*

The major premise behind Parental Intelligence is that a child's behavior
or misbehavior has meaning—and often more than one. Once the trea-
sure trove of meanings emerges, we realize that there are many possible
reactions to misbehavior. If these ideas are new and even challenging to
you, the following journey will take you to a positive and satisfying stage
in your parenting life. Learning these new concepts is like acquiring a
fresh mental toolbox that requires the same focus as learning anything
new, and you may experience the same discomfort that comes with acquiring any new skill.

Think of learning to dance. Before learning the first step, you need
to develop the right mindset. Most people who want to learn how to
dance have an open mind. They want to learn new steps and, therefore,
approach the task with a positive attitude. However, if they are overly
self-conscious, they may develop resistance to the new steps that will
jeopardize the learning process. Instead, they may need to deliber-
ately develop the outlook that learning to dance could be worthwhile.
Hopefully, when the music transports them, they will enter the dance
floor with a new frame of mind.

Once the hopeful dancer establishes an open mindset, the process of
learning to dance can begin. At first, each movement is very conscious
and deliberate. How far do I turn my body? How much do I stretch in

time with the beat? How much momentum do I need to get my arms and legs to turn in different ways? How much do I engage with my partner as I move in one direction or the other? How do I manage all this while maintaining some grace and even charm? Most importantly: How do I end the dance in concert with my partner?

Once learned and practiced, all these little movements eventually combine into a seamless choreography that allows dancers to negotiate the dance floor as if it were second nature. Without much thought, dancers become able to perform on a large dance floor, in a small space, under bright lights, and in the dark. Over time, skills become increasingly automatic and nuanced. What felt uncertain becomes secure. Forever, there are new situations—tests, in a way—when dancers need to adjust and maneuver in uncharted ways, but they have internalized the basic core of dancing.

Learning a new parenting approach requires a similar process. While learning to parent and learning to dance clearly are two different skills, both involve learning through relating to someone else. Some dancers perform with their bodies in close proximity; others prefer distance. Some dancers are very spirited, while others move slowly in time. Some dancers are aggressive and bold, while others are subtle and gentle. There are infinite styles of dance, and each pair has to find their own—together. The same is true for parents and children—style, timing, and rhythm need to work for everyone involved. The parent who wants to raise children must first have the mindset that there are many ways to carry out the multifaceted task of childrearing effectively, depending on the individual personalities of both parent and child.

Imagine yourself in a situation where your child is repeating a misbehavior for which you have punished him in the past. What happened? You already punished him for that—why is it happening again? Instead of seeing this as a disaster, see it as an opportunity. Pause and make use of this moment of uncertainty. While such perplexity may feel overwhelming, recognize this state of confusion as part of the journey, signaling that you are in transition and that a new phase of parenting has begun.

This important parenting mindset is founded on the belief that external behavior has internal causes. Parents and children alike behave based on what they think and feel. Using my approach, parents begin to learn how to hold in mind their own thoughts and feelings as well as their child's thoughts and feelings simultaneously.

What does this mean? In this book, you will read about the concept of "holding someone in mind." For the untutored parent, usually that "someone" is herself. Accordingly, when a child "misbehaves," mothers or fathers may think that the child is doing something to them personally and react based on that belief ("She's just causing me trouble, and now I'm mad."). However, after learning my methods, the parent will be able to think not only about her own reactions to the misbehavior, but also about the child's internal experience when the misbehavior occurred. The child's experience may not be about doing something to the parent by misbehaving, but instead may be about communicating something to the parent that was brewing inside the child.

Let's fast forward to two of the parents and children you will meet in this book: Clive and his father, and Olivia and her mother. Let's assume that Clive's father and Olivia's mother have completed this book and have acquired a secure parenting mindset.

One morning, when Clive's father told him to put on his shoes to get ready for school, the six-year-old threw them across the room. Clive's father learned a great deal about parenting by following a series of steps about effective parenting (which will soon become apparent as we get to know him later). Therefore, he was able to experience Clive's impulsive reaction and his own annoyance with Clive's behavior simultaneously. He learned that holding both his and Clive's feelings in mind was a requisite for understanding what may be going on when they are working at cross purposes.

He wanted Clive to get ready for school, but he didn't know yet that Clive didn't even want to go to school, something that had never happened before. Clive's father knew he had to look for meaning behind his son's behavior. He understood that if he jumped in and insisted that Clive put the shoes on immediately, he might miss an important opportunity at real and true communication. He held back from giving an immediate consequence to Clive's action. He held his breath and forced himself to wait for Clive to calm down.

Because he and Clive had worked on this approach for months, Clive's father was able to ask Clive if something was upsetting him about putting on his shoes to get ready for school. Eventually, Clive was able to explain what was bothering him. Clive told his dad that during an arithmetic lesson in his kindergarten class, he gave a wrong answer to a simple addition problem and a classmate laughed. In response, Clive poked the boy with the eraser end of his pencil. The boy cried out and the teacher, who is generally quite sensitive to kindhearted Clive, took a most unusual but spontaneous action—she yelled at him. Clive didn't know that was the reason he threw the shoes, but his father was able to make the connection in his mind.

The father's awareness that his child's impulsive behavior must have a reason enabled him to take a step back and create space for Clive to explain what happened at school the day before. The parenting mindset that asks the parent to hold both himself and his child in mind creates a sense of safety for both child and parent. An atmosphere of safety allows children to communicate feelings and events that are most distressing, exciting, and important to them without embarrassment or self-consciousness. Using Parental Intelligence, misbehavior becomes a catalyst for communication.

On the way to the kitchen, thirteen-year-old Olivia said to her mother, who was not yet in sight, "Mommy, I have something to tell you, but I don't want you to be mad." Implementing the principles of Parental Intelligence, her mother immediately adopted the nonjudgmental, empathic mindset needed to help Olivia feel safe enough to talk to her.

"Whatever it is," her mother said, "we can work it out."

Olivia, head down, walked into the kitchen where she raised her face to show her mother a golden ring piercing her lower lip. Her mother was shocked, but she worked hard at reserving her feelings, holding Olivia's worry in mind as well. It was important to Olivia's mother that Olivia could tell her about this without fearing her reaction. Olivia started to cry and explained that her best friend convinced her to go to the mall where they each got a lip ring. At first, they thought it would be fun to have a new look, but as soon as it was done, they knew it was a big mistake.

"How big a mistake could this be?" Olivia's mother asked. "If you don't want to leave it in, take it out, and the hole will close up in a few days."

Even though Olivia already knew this, her mother's response allowed her to experience her mother as a safe parent, someone she could approach with her problems. She and her mother discussed as openly as they could why Olivia experimented with the lip piercing, learning together that there may be several reasons. Olivia wanted to feel prettier: her self-image was uncertain, and she wanted to experiment with a new look that she thought was more mature. She also wanted to do something independently from her mother. The conversation with her mother allowed her to feel her mother's acceptance, which, in turn, supported her attempt at independence, even though it didn't turn out well. Keeping her shock to herself, Olivia's mother reaped tremendous rewards. She learned much more about Olivia than she had imagined was possible, and she suffered along with her daughter as Olivia poured out her lack of confidence and desire to be independent.

Olivia's mother knew that keeping both herself and her daughter in mind would provide the safe environment her daughter needed to truthfully explain what had happened. This led to greater understanding, not only of this experience, but also of their relationship as a whole. The sense of safety between Olivia and her mother didn't come with this one incident, but with hundreds of such encounters in everyday life. As we shall soon see, this was a huge accomplishment for Olivia's mother. She had overcome many of her own fears by the time of this incident and was able to contain them to help her daughter.

Let's think for a moment what might have happened if Clive's father and Olivia's mother had not learned Parental Intelligence and only held their own reactions in mind. It is likely that their children would not have felt comfortable sharing their stories. For example, if Clive's father only felt his own annoyance, he might have rushed a distressed Clive to put his shoes on, and Clive would have cried. This might have annoyed Clive's father even more, and he might have yelled at Clive for being a bad boy, something Clive most certainly did not want to be. Clive might have gone to school even more upset and had trouble functioning well in kindergarten that day. Clive wouldn't have found he could trust his father with his worries, and the issue at school would never have been understood and resolved.

In the second example, if Olivia's mother had not used the parenting approach explained in this book and held a different parenting mindset, she might have expressed her shock when she saw Olivia's lip ring. She probably would have yelled at her for using such poor judgment, told her she looked awful, and punished her. She never would have found out Olivia's regret for her action and all the reasons why she did it that pertained to her self-esteem. Olivia and her mother would have created a schism in their relationship, and Olivia would have felt very alone with her problems.

Clearly, the approach Clive's father and Olivia's mother used was quite successful. Their parenting mindset embraced the challenge of conflict, and they were open to gaining insight from the behaviors before them. They understood the feelings of their children and the meanings behind their behaviors, so they could help their children resolve their problems. However, a parent cannot always know exactly when, what, and how to listen and react, so the appropriate response may not always be clear or ready at hand. Children can sense, perhaps ambivalently at first, when a parent's mindset ensures a sense of safety in the relationship. As time goes on, the child trusts and values the safety she feels with her parent. Subsequently, the child learns how to identify other safe people to choose to be with in her life, and she, too, becomes someone who can create an atmosphere of safety for others.

Parents may discover that they need to ascribe multiple possible meanings to the behavior in question. For example, Clive threw his shoes for two reasons. First, he didn't want to go to school since the teacher had yelled at him the day before. At the same time, he *did* want to go to school and be viewed as a good boy. Parents can and must expect not only multiple meanings behind a behavior, but sometimes contradictory meanings as well (wanting and not wanting to go to school).

Not only may one behavior have several meanings, several behaviors may have one and the same meaning. The day Clive was yelled at, he resisted doing his homework. This was unusual for him; Clive usually enjoyed doing homework on his own, without any prompts from his father. This time, however, his father sat with him while he worked on his arithmetic, which seemed to help.

The next morning, after the shoe incident and Clive's explanation, his father linked the different behaviors—protesting homework and throwing shoes—to the incident in school. He now understood the meanings behind Clive's behaviors. Clive didn't want to do his homework because he'd had enough of school that day. While Clive usually enjoyed doing homework on his own, which his father understood made him feel like an older kid who was proud of himself, this time his father intuitively offering to sit with him had given him the comfort he needed.

These examples show that a parent is not only responding to physical, but also to psychological reality. Throwing the shoes or getting the lip ring constituted physical reality. Clive's desire to be liked by his teacher, to be a good child, to not be embarrassed at school, and for his father to

take his side constituted Clive's psychological reality. Olivia's psychological reality included her fear of making her mother angry, her worry over
her self-image, and her wish to do something independently.

These examples highlight the importance of how parents construe
behavior. Think of moiré fabric. It is actually flat, but it looks like something is moving. If you take two ordinary screens and move one over
the other, it creates the same effect. Or picture a birdwatcher who sees a
figure in the sky. He assumes it's a hawk. He's enchanted. Then he has a
sense of dissonance and self-doubt. Upon closer inspection, he discovers
it is a fly in front of his glasses. Behavior can be this way. Depending on
how it is construed, it can propel you into a series of presumptions that
are right on or can lead you astray.

Depending on the template you use, what you see can be interpreted
from many vantage points. A template is a metaphor for a behavior from
which you make presumptions and draw conclusions that may be accurate or misleading. Clive's father and Olivia's mother held their views at
bay until they understood the vantage points most accurate for understanding their children's behaviors. However, untutored parents may
not do this. They may fall prey to their first guess at what an action is all
about instead of considering competing explanations for an unwanted
behavior.

For example, parents are meaning-makers as they design wide variations in their sensory metaphors for ordinary misbehaviors. Imagine
these snapshots of competing metaphors. A temper tantrum is a raging
hailstorm, a misfired rocket, a lightning bolt, a tornado, a whirling der-
vish, boiling water letting off steam, or a lost soul dissolving into tears.
A messy room is a train wreck, a battlefield, or a disorganized mind.
Hitting a sibling is a sniper act, a missile launcher, or a blow to a scorned
rival. Missing curfew is the act of a culprit, the waging of a rebellion, or a
flight into growing independence. Repetitive, loud singing is a dripping
faucet, a broken record, a buzz saw, a screeching owl, or a hummingbird
soothing his flock.

Depending on the parents' metaphor for their child's behavior, they will act and react in different ways. With an open-minded parenting mindset, these presumptions become evident. Parents need to look at the way they are thinking and feeling from a distance. It is important to go far beyond the appearances of behaviors from the visual images they call to mind to the subtle depths of what they represent. Thus, as a parent, you do not just think and feel, but you also observe your process of thinking and feeling. Clive's father and Olivia's mother look back on their interactions with their children, go over the communications that took place, and feel proud of their interactions and understandings.

In summary, there are many interwoven characteristics of the parenting mindset:

- Finding internal causes to external behaviors
- Holding both yourself and your child in mind
- Developing an atmosphere of safety
- Looking for multiple meanings behind behaviors
- Separating physical reality from psychological reality
- Observing your parenting process from a distance

Parental Intelligence is flexible and creative, yet it always includes a wish for insight. Once insight is gained, decisions can be made.

Summary

This parenting mindset can and will affect your daily life and give you and your child a greater sense of well-being. Olivia and her mother felt safe and comfortable enough to be discussing Olivia's problems. This reinforced their relationship, giving them a feeling of strength and comfort within themselves and a feeling of being grounded and secure. Olivia's mother's self-image as an effective parent grew, and Olivia's self-image as a daughter who can safely experiment and trust her mother despite a mistake was affirmed. Clive and his father felt a strong connection because Clive's empathic father recognized and understood Clive's important conflicts. Both children felt accepted by their parents as they worked out their troubles together.

Parental Intelligence allows a hopeful outlook. You are ready to learn the steps that are necessary to evolve as effective and loving parents who listen to their children through words and actions. This orientation, once established, stays inside of you.

Chapter Two

What Fuels Punishment Instead of a Search for Meaning?

Faced with unwanted behavior? First ask,
"What does it mean?" not "What do I do?"

As parents, we try to make sense of our child's world. When their lives impinge on us and we slowly discover and assemble the truth, our children's behaviors sometimes tell a story that presents a challenge and new questions arise. We have expectations that haven't been met and grow tired. We need a behind-the-scenes look at the real face of their actions—but that takes time. For some inexplicable reason, we imagine we don't have that time and rush to punish away the misdeeds.

In the face of reality, I offer two ideas: (1) behaviors have underlying meanings; and (2) once meaning is clear, options other than punishment will surface that are more effective. In this chapter, I focus on what compels parents to punish misbehavior rather than first seeking to understand what motivates their child's actions. I address this theme because if parents slow down long enough to trace the story behind their child's behavior, they will reach a preferred outcome. In this way, parents can gain the advantage of knowing who their child really is while renewing their faith in their youngster and in themselves as parents.

Parents punish in the hope of achieving aims that all parents share:

- Keeping their children safe (believing that punishment will deter their children from behaving in dangerous or self-destructive ways)

- Raising their children to be socially responsible (believing that punishment will correct children from being inconsiderate of others)
- Helping their children develop self-discipline and self-control (believing that punishment will encourage children to do their best to achieve well-defined goals)

All these objectives reflect responsible parenting; the question is how to achieve them. Discipline involves teaching and giving knowledge; however, it is too often equated with punishment and control. So, let's take a closer look at what punishment consists of.

For this discussion, let's define punishment as an action taken or imposed on a child in reaction to a child's behavior contrary to a parent's rule or moral belief. It's common for caring parents to use punishment to try to curb current misbehavior and to deter future misbehavior. Their wishes make sense, but their methods, though well-meant, don't accomplish their aims. In my work with parents and their children, I have found, in fact, that punishment often does not help parents achieve those objectives. Instead, understanding that misbehavior hints at struggles lying below the surface of unwanted behaviors can help parents raise children who are safe, considerate, social, and well disciplined.

Punishment can take many forms, some more controlled than others. Controlled examples of punishment include grounding, time-out or taking away toys, computers, cell phones, and privileges. Parents who implement such punishments may feel their authority and pride is at stake, and unless they intervene quickly, a precedent will be set, the misbehavior will escalate, and the parent will lose the child's respect.

Some less-controlled examples of punishment include a belief in talion revenge (an eye for an eye; you hit me, so I hit you to show you how it feels), screaming, silent treatment, banishing a child to be alone in a room for an extended period of time, threats, humiliation, and other acts that are beyond the child's ability to tolerate emotionally. However well-intentioned, some punishments border on bullying, given that the child is small and feels helpless, while the adult is large and feels powerful and righteous. Outright physical or emotional abuse is beyond the scope of this discussion.

When rethinking punishment and looking for meaning behind behavior, let's start with emotions. Our emotions serve us well if we take time to understand their origins, but if we don't, they can lead us, as parents, to assign ineffective punishments. This happens when we show the right emotion (disapproval) but with exaggerated intensity (screaming or silent treatment) or in a harmful way (hitting). Our concern may have been justified, but we overreacted, got too fearful, and threatened or carried out a punishment unproductively. While the anger or frustration may have been warranted, the response becomes counterproductive if there was no consideration of the meaning behind the behavior.

In households where strict punishment is the rule, children learn to be afraid and to avoid punishment, not to behave appropriately. When punishments are excessive—that is, if the punishment is beyond the child's ability to tolerate it or if it is unrelated to the unacceptable behavior—the child cannot understand and appreciate the connection between crime and punishment. As a result, the child's future behavior is dictated by fear alone. It may seem as if moral learning has taken place, but in fact what has been learned is avoidance behavior. Future behavior is guided by fear—"How do I manage things so that I do not get punished?"—not by insight—"I guess Daddy's right, and I won't do that again."

Furthermore, punishment "pays" for a child's mistakes and absolves the child on a superficial and external level rather than building a conscience that creates an inner guide for future behavior. Instead of teaching a lesson in morality, punishment leads to hurt and resentment, which may sometimes even worsen the misbehavior because the child is angry and doesn't feel understood.

I have found that many parents have been conditioned to respond to anger with anger, to react to disrespect with further disrespect, often leading to rapid punishment before the actual situation has been examined. The idea that behavior has meaning isn't even in the picture. Furthermore, sometimes we have blind spots to our children's emotions. We can be misled by their actions, draw erroneous conclusions about the intentions behind them, and punish unnecessarily. In many cases, our experiences lead us to believe that the situation would threaten our child's welfare and that punishment is necessary.

Parents' past experiences may fuel their approach to punishment. Some parents use the same methods of punishment their parents used because they feel they were raised appropriately. When these parents rely on such punitive measures, too, their parents (the child's grandparents) encourage it. Punishment is attractive because quick action gives an immediate feeling of control. Ironically, parents sometimes reenact the type of punishment they experienced as children, forgetting the negative consequences they felt as children. Other parents who grew up with strict discipline may be determined not to repeat the past, but because these measures are so deeply embedded, they may fall back on them and consider them "just necessary" sometimes.

Some parents who were punished as children may find themselves in the grasp of a complicated dynamic. If they were spanked or hit or given silent treatment, their anger and hurt is sometimes still quite alive, but at other times, these emotions have become a deep, dark wound. Without realizing it, parents can end up taking out their anger and hurt on their children, as if they could get back at their parents through their children. Their unconscious is at play; past and present are confused. When the child reminds parents of their own parents, mothers and fathers may become overwhelmed and lose their equilibrium.

For example, when your teen doesn't listen to you repeatedly about finishing homework before turning on his iPod, you may unconsciously recall the hurt from your childhood when your mother didn't listen to you for years on end.

Feeling ineffective, you complain to your best friend, "I've been screaming at him every day this week. Why won't he just listen to me? He gets so difficult. He says he's going to do his work, but then closes his door and switches on his iPod or a video. He's fourteen. He's known the homework rule since first grade. I'd take the computer away, but he needs to email his assignments to his teachers. So, I take away a party this weekend. He scowls at me, but it doesn't change anything. Help!"

Your friend replies wisely, "I know how difficult it is for you. But, if you don't mind a comment, maybe he's old enough now to manage his time himself. He's a good student. He usually does listen to you. Maybe he needs downtime after school before doing his homework. When you took away the party, he missed seeing that girl you told me about."

Past and present mixed and mingled. This parent lost the clear image of her son until her friend tried to revive it for her. She got confused when her feelings about not being listened to took center stage, and she punished her son needlessly. She started to overreact by screaming at him, striking back as if he were her mother not listening to her from the past.

Parents misconstrue their children's misbehavior for other reasons, too. They often punish when they feel that the child's misbehavior is directed at them. They may be angry but are mostly hurt. Emotions again! They want to get back at the child, to show him or her how the injury feels, believing that such retaliation will prevent the child from further misbehavior or disrespect. However, the child will likely feel angrier, which may escalate or even promote the misbehavior. As a result, the cycle repeats. Even if the child does not misbehave again, he or she surely will feel alienated, and consequently, the parent-child relationship falls apart.

Sometimes parents' intentions and expectations are clear, but sometimes they are not. Punishment itself doesn't make goals clear or teach right from wrong. Parenting with an interest in understanding the meaning of behavior depends on teaching children what they need to know, what the rules are, and what parents expect. Such parenting does not require punishment; it involves teaching, promoting learning, giving knowledge, and understanding the hallmarks of good discipline.

Punishing children for not following rules, for example, may occur when the rules no longer apply to a child who has outgrown them or because the rules no longer fit a changed situation and need to be revised. Blindly punishing such a disobeyed rule wouldn't teach right from wrong but would more likely lead to distrust between parent and child—not effective discipline.

Here's another example. Let's say a child overreacts by screaming and disturbing others after being told playtime will be over in fifteen minutes because dinner is almost ready. A parent might want to punish or "discipline" with a time-out. Time for the child to regain inner self-control and collect himself is warranted, a necessary goal, but the time-out could be explained to the child as a time to slow down and think for a little while before finishing playing. This is using discipline to teach something essential in a positive way with brief, but clearly explained motives. The parent might even sit with the child during the time-out to help him learn how to calm down. This isn't punishment. It is reasonably giving the child a way to regain self-control and self-discipline so he can later understand the rules of how to talk and not yell at others when he is disappointed. In fact, he may follow his parent's helpful strategy and give himself time-outs in the future by removing himself from situations to give himself a chance to think things through—a valuable way to retain inner control, which he learned from his parents' non-punitive approach.

However, my experience from years of listening to parents and children tells me that children usually do know what is right and wrong. Punishment doesn't teach it; they already know. Something else is amiss.

Summary

Punishment is an action taken or imposed on a child in reaction to a child's behavior contrary to a parent's rule or moral belief. In many situations, punishments—or threats of punishments—are used in the hope of changing the unwanted behavior or preventing future misbehavior.

However, in the end, when punishment is threatened or tried, solutions to problems do not follow.

Parents who jump to punishment in reaction to misbehavior are not following a course of action that helps them understand that their children's misbehaviors have underlying meanings. Although the parents are well-intentioned, they focus only on the misbehaviors and their immediate consequences. It's counterintuitive not to give immediate consequences for misbehavior, but parents would be wise to remember the old adage "think before you act." Parents who resort to punishment are reacting with insufficient information about the reasons for and causes behind the behaviors, and they are forgetting about their relationship with their children.

Many steps lie between misbehavior and solution—five, to be precise. The next chapter will outline the five-step process that encompasses Parental Intelligence.

Chapter Three

Five Steps to Parental Intelligence

Misbehavior carries a message.
It's not a solo act.
It is an invitation for understanding.

While individual parents all face unique challenges, I have discovered many commonalities that affect their varied situations. To parent effectively, I have developed five powerfully valuable steps that allow every parent—no matter how different their circumstances—to find meaning behind their child's behavior and, beyond that, to intelligently and compassionately resolve the underlying problems.

The five steps to Parental Intelligence are:

1. Stepping Back
2. Self-Reflecting
3. Understanding Your Child's Mind
4. Understanding Your Child's Development
5. Problem Solving

Together, these five steps provide a road map to help you get to your destination: the place where you understand the meaning behind your child's behavior. What was once obscure will become clear. When the meaning or meanings behind the behavior are understood, it is much easier to decide the best ways to handle the situation. Although the unfolding steps are described in sequence, it is valuable to go back and forth among them as you unlock your Parental Intelligence. Especially when handling the problem-solving step, self-reflecting and understanding your child's mind are often repeated. As new information comes to light, empathy between you and your child will deepen. Going through the five-step process with your child often uncovers problems that are of greater significance than the original misbehavior. What had been unspeakable will become known, and a new and stronger alliance will form between you and your child.

STEP ONE
Stepping Back

A parent's first reaction to misbehavior is often emotional. Without distancing themselves from their emotional response, parents often make rash decisions that lead to punishments they later regret because they do not achieve the desired results. Responding effectively means starting from the same emotional place, which may be uncomfortable, but making it a priority to step back, tolerate the child's feelings, and gradually shift to a more reasoned response will lead to a better outcome.

Imagine taking a video of the incident of misbehavior, rewinding it, and playing it back in slow motion to get a more detailed picture of what occurred. This means tracking the misbehavior and giving it a beginning, middle, and end. Thinking this way allows you to recall what happened before the incident—what your child did, what you did, and how you felt. While having information doesn't mean you know what to do with it, it does set the stage for future, more enlightened parenting choices.

Stepping back requires opening up your thinking and allowing yourself to experience a wide range of emotions without taking immediate action. Sometimes, after an incident, parents feel anxious, on edge, and restless, and will immediately jump into action to alleviate these feelings. Sometimes parents refrain from acting impulsively but feel a nagging tension that interferes with their ability to see the situation objectively. Such a parent may be stuck in one point of view or focus solely on a specific but incomplete set of details. It is not always enough to replay an event, because the replay may confirm or intensify the original emotion. For stepping back to be effective, a parent must replay the event while also trying to understand the original emotions the event provoked in him or her.

The process of stepping back also includes the suspension of judgment. This allows you to take time to figure out what happened before taking action. If you never pause, you never allow emotions to subside and thinking to begin. Stepping back prepares you to engage in the parenting mindset that says what happened is meaningful. Even in an emergency, once the immediate situation has been handled, there is room for refraining from ready conclusions and for stepping back.

Some people are primarily inwardly directed and tend to think things through. But not all thinking is productive reasoning; without sufficient information, thoughts might well be going in circles. A parent may be reluctant to review and rethink his or her original reaction for fear of appearing soft or inadequate or inconsistent. Other people are primarily outwardly directed and focused on what is going on around them, excluding their own and their child's inner feelings and thoughts when they are trying to understand their child's misbehavior. There may be a reluctance to go inside oneself to experience emotions, for fear of feeling out of control.

Stepping back requires slowing down and thinking about what just happened and how you feel about it, suspending not only judgment about your child's behavior, but also about your parenting behavior. Stepping back gives the parent permission to not always know what to do. Consequently, when a parent reacts one way on the spot, but later understands what happened more fully, he or she can feel confident returning to the child with new thoughts and feelings that, though once restricted, have begun to expand, offering a new perspective.

When you step back, you prepare yourself to recognize that behaviors have many causes. By pausing, you give yourself time to compare the last time the behavior happened to the present situation. You may discover a pattern in your interaction with your child and begin to wonder, *Are there many causes for the behavior that I couldn't consider at the time?* You may then begin to see the behavior in its many aspects: What triggered the behavior? How long did it last? When did it escalate or decrease? You may also begin to see facets of the behavior, facets you were blind to because of the high emotional states during the incident. Once you are in the mode of seeking full knowledge of what happened, you will begin to discover that several problems might be involved in the misbehavior.

Once you calm down, you begin to notice expressions on your child's face, the words your child said, your child's gestures and postures, and your child's mood and shifts in feelings. After a while, this one behavior can be broken down and understood as many separate behaviors. Stepping back can open up your mind to such an extent that it almost feels like a different behavior or group of behaviors than what you originally assumed.

Stepping back gives you space and time to evaluate the situation, examine and question assumptions, and realize that the situation isn't fully understood. Take as much time as you need to consider what is happening. In your mind, say to yourself, *Slo-o-o-w down. Take your time. Hold on. Don't thrust forward. Resist those impulses. Breathe deeply. Sit quietly. Consider what to say or do, if anything.*

Both mothers and fathers invested in the process—not just the outcomes—of child rearing have a greater tendency to naturally learn to step back. Fathers and mothers can encourage and help each other in stepping back, particularly in two-parent households where co-parenting is a goal. Parents who live in separate residences but have ongoing relationships with their child and share in co-parenting are also more likely to find stepping back a good alternative to impulsive reactions as they learn how to balance their responsibilities for both work and childcare. The significance of mothers and fathers supporting each other in the process of stepping back cannot be underestimated. A mother may be the buffer to a father's automatic release of anger, just as he may do the same for her.

When you give yourself permission to slow down before reacting and deciding on consequences, you can reduce stress and feel more in control. Stepping back changes the tone between parent and child. When children see their parents taking their time, they start to feel, perhaps cautiously at first, that their parents can be trusted to guide them.

Summary of Stepping Back

The purpose of stepping back is to set the stage for parents to take stock of their feelings and organize their thinking about what occurred. This is just common sense, but it requires tolerating frustration—a skill we are hoping to also teach our children. While thinking over what occurred, parents ideally suspend judgment and acknowledge that misbehavior carries meaning. This is the first step in this parenting approach that accepts the concept that the "misbehavior" communicates a child's feelings and motives and may indicate problems that need to be solved in the parent-child relationship.

The next step, self-reflecting, increases parents' ability to understand their own feelings and motives that led to their actions following what they thought was simply "misbehavior."

STEP TWO
Self-Reflecting

Self-reflecting allows you to discover how your past affects your present approach to parenting. Self-reflecting allows you to observe yourself objectively and think about the genesis of your feelings, motives, and actions in both present and previous relationships. This step requires honestly questioning why you behaved the way you did. Sounds logical, but I know it can be hard. It's so tempting to just jump to ready solutions and skip questioning what's going on inside of you.

For parents, self-reflecting is an extension of stepping back. It requires you to consider what led to your specific responses to your child's behavior, prompts you to think about your actions from many perspectives, and allows you to consider many causes for your response to your child's misbehavior. That sounds like a tall order, but if you take it bit by bit, it's amazing what you discover.

Self-reflecting happens after the incident, maybe hours or days later. Sometimes it is subtle. You're in your car at a red light, and your mind returns to the situation. By considering your reactions, you suddenly see them from a different perspective.

You discuss the situation and your reactions specifically with a friend or a spouse, and they offer new perspectives on your reactions. Other times you purposefully rethink the problem behavior and ask yourself if there are other ways to approach the situation or if you could mirror the ways you've seen other parents react to similar situations.

You begin to question, *Why did I react that particular way, now that I see it wasn't the only way?* or *What were my motives and intentions?* or *What in my past affected my thinking and actions in the present?* or *What were my emotional reactions to my child's behavior, and where did they come from?*

If you allow yourself to take your time, this isn't as difficult as you might imagine. In fact, you notice that you're beginning to feel more confident. Self-reflecting is a discovery process. You are getting to know yourself better. It feels good. Self-reflecting allows you to learn more about yourself as a child and teenager, and about the effect your experiences may have had on your present reactions to your child.

Self-reflecting often leads to a realization that you take your child's actions very personally. That's hard to accept, but it's also relieving to understand. You realize that sometimes you feel persecuted by your child; you want to be the boss, yet your child has control. Then you reflect further and consider how to be authoritative, yet kind and compassion-ately involved in your child's life. This takes a strong sense of self—a capacity for self-awareness. You are already feeling better about yourself.

Your relationships with your own caregivers during infancy, child-hood, and adolescence, which may include parents, teachers, and other adults, may determine your capacity for reflective functioning as an adult. These early experiences shape the expectations of future attach-ments. When you bring your own conflicts from the past to the forefront and understand them, it helps you to help your child.

Admittedly, patterns of relationships are often unconscious and difficult to change without therapeutic intervention. Nonetheless, even if parents seek treatment, they can't just wait for their therapy to end before they help their child; their child continues to grow and needs help now. It can be surprisingly effective for parents to realize that their thoughts and reactions can come from the past and affect the specific behavior in question.

Think of a distressing behavior your child exhibits. Consider your feelings during the incident. Now go back and find a past experience that triggered the same or similar feelings. Review it slowly, like a story, in as much detail as you can. Think about the people in your life at that time and what they meant to you, then and now. You may find that your child's present behavior triggers aspects from that past situation.

Ask yourself some questions: Does my child's behavior remind me of my behavior in the past? Does my child's behavior remind me of some-one else's behavior in the past? Was my past situation a marker for me in some way? Was the past situation a turning point in my life? Do I have unresolved feelings about that time? As you go through this mental and emotional process, you may begin remembering more and more. Thoughts and details that were hidden for years begin to surface. All of these memories may very well have to do with the way you now react to your child.

There are several possibilities. If your child's behavior, manner, pos-ture, or tone of voice resonate with how you interacted with someone else at earlier times in your life, you may be reacting to your child the way you reacted when you were younger. That's very enlightening. Or you may be reacting to your child the way you wished you had reacted when you were younger. Now you are really getting somewhere. Light bulbs are going off. Your mind is racing backward, and you are feeling much more in touch with your reactions. Alternatively, it may be that someone reacted to you the way your child is behaving now, and that is what's so upsetting to you. Past and present have converged. No wonder you reacted so strongly.

Your capacity for self-reflection may grow as your child grows. If your child reaches an age that was troublesome for you when you were young, conflict between you and your child may ensue because you are reminded of your unresolved problems at that age. Realizing that you dealt with similar issues opens up your understanding by leaps and bounds. Maybe it takes a lifetime to become adept at self-reflecting, but as you're learning, you can improve your relationship with your child.

There are many past stereotypes about women being more empathic and tuned into feelings than men, which could affect their capacity to self-reflect. However, in thirty years of experience with many different parents, I have not seen a gender preference for self-reflecting. I have, however, found that men's past experiences with their fathers when they were children affect what they expect of themselves as fathers. They either want to give their children the same positive experiences they had or they want to give their children better fathering experiences than they had. Both women and men whose fathers were not active in their lives may have low expectations for the father's involvement with their children. Women with such low expectations may be surprised and pleased when their children's fathers want to be invested in parenting. In fact, this may have been part of what attracted them to these men. Likewise, men who did not have close relationships with their fathers may wish to provide more closeness with their children. Similarly, women may have experienced their mothers' involvement with them as children as something they want to emulate or change when they become mothers. When parents engage in self-reflecting, these yearnings come to light and have a positive effect on the children.

Summary of Self-Reflecting

As parents understand themselves better through self-reflecting, they become more consciously aware of the impact their past has on their present responses to their children in specific situations. As a result, punishment can recede into the background, while alternative reactions come to mind that are far more effective than just handling a specific singular transgression. Parental self-reflecting leads to new levels of compassion and resilience in parent-child relationships. Stepping back and self-reflecting add great depth to understanding your current reactions to your child.

Self-reflecting helps mothers and fathers question why they react in punitive ways instead of searching for meaning. Parental impulsive reactions that lead to punishment wane, creating a readiness for flexible, sensitized decision-making. Insightful decision-making builds bridges to your child that lead to understanding your child's mind—Step Three in this parenting approach.

STEP THREE
Understanding Your Child's Mind

"What's on your mind?" is a question often asked casually, but understanding your child's mind is central to knowing your child. This casual question prompts a series of other questions about parenting. How is the mind of an infant different from the mind of a child? Does understanding the mind of a child help the child cope? Does understanding the mind of a child help you cope? And what roles do emotions play in your child's thinking?

Understanding your child's mind starts with knowing your child's mental states. What are they? The term *mental state* refers to all mental experiences. A short list of mental states would include intentions, thoughts, desires, wishes, beliefs, and feelings. Contradictory and diverse mental states can occur at the same time. For example, a teen wishes (a mental state) to have ice cream, and yet he feels he shouldn't because he intends (a mental state) to lose weight so he can make the wrestling team.

When I talk about mental states, I am also referring to physical states, because they are inextricably interwoven. This can be especially seen in an infant. An infant has a mind with feelings and desires. How does the attentive mother notice these mental states? When the baby feels hungry (a mental state), he may lick his lips with his tongue. The mother knows to nurse him. She observes contentment (another mental state) when the baby releases the nipple and falls asleep.

Your ability to understand your child's mind is directly related to your ability to self-reflect. As described above, self-reflecting is your capacity to think about your own experiences throughout life. Self-awareness and awareness of the mental states of others are closely linked. When, with self-reflecting, you are able to understand how your own mind is working, you also realize that your child's mind is separate and autonomous from yours. However, if you do not understand this, you may attribute your own mental states (intentions and feelings) to your child.

For example, let's say you are angry at your ten-year-old for being curt with you. It's breakfast time, and you laid out a balanced, delicious meal for him on the kitchen table: toast with his favorite jam, granola, and his favorite fruit-juice smoothie—the works! However, he barely says, "Good morning," grabs a piece of toast, and runs out the door. You feel disrespected. He barely noticed what you'd done. You're angry he wasn't grateful for the lovely meal you prepared. You assume he was mad at you from the quick, "See ya," he called without even looking at you. His anger was completely unjustified. The assumption is simple: you're angry; he's angry. You've forgotten that your child's feelings and intentions may be quite different from your own. In this example, what actually happened, you find out later, was your child was curt because he was late for the school bus. He was in a hurry. He wasn't mad at you at all.

Here's another example. A child is frustrated when the dinner in a restaurant isn't served quickly and complains vigorously that he's starving. His father, however, had a big lunch, is enjoying everyone's company, and doesn't mind waiting. He finds his fifteen-year-old son's complaints rude and scolds him, telling him to quiet down or he can't go out later. The son feels resentful. Their mental states—their intentions and feelings—are different. His father mistakenly assumed that what is on his mind is also on his son's mind.

Such inability to be aware that one's own mental state is different from that of one's child can lead a parent to misinterpret the intent of the child's behavior, causing a rupture in the parent-child relationship and, sometimes, unnecessary punishment.

Understanding your child's mind depends on realizing the links between intentions, feelings, thoughts, and behaviors, and looking for meanings behind behaviors. Behaviors and feelings are inextricably bound together.

For instance, a mother might say to her son, "You punched the wall when your brother took your baseball mitt without asking. He's been doing this for weeks, and your frustration has reached its limit. Think about it. I bet by hitting the wall, you were avoiding hitting him."

Now that she's planted a new idea in her son's mind, she continues, "Let's think and talk more about your frustration, so you don't ever need to punch a wall." She's now connected his emotion—frustration—to his behavior—punching.

A parent who approaches the situation like that is attuned to what's going on in his or her child's mind that caused the behavior. While the father in the example in the restaurant above was unable to shift from a punitive stance to understanding his child's mind, this mother links her son's internal emotional state to his behavior.

Most parents and children can recognize each other's moods but need time to figure out the reason for a particular mood. Behavior is meaningful, even if you don't catch on right away. Often, you need to let the behavior sit in your mind, waiting for its meaning to emerge. This is stepping back. If, as a parent, you know your child very well and have been trying to understand his or her mind for many years, over many developmental stages, you can become quite an expert at reading your child's moods and thoughts.

Of course, it's important to check your ideas with your child. This shows empathy: "It seems like your feelings were hurt by the teacher, so you bolted out of the classroom. Was it something like that?"

Let's say your child reveals she is feeling hurt. After hearing your child's response, you might continue: "Now that we can figure out what was going on in your mind, were there other choices you may have had, so that you can react another way next time you feel hurt?"

No one likes being instructed on how they should feel, but it sure feels good to be understood. Everyone appreciates empathy. Feeling understood can help a child contain his emotions and begin to think them through. When a child feels his parent understands what is going on inside his mind, he feels attended to and supported, and then can think further about how to handle situations.

It's important to realize, however, that all parents have had experiences growing up that caused the formation of emotional triggers that still exist in the present, often unconsciously. These triggers prompt responses to their children's behaviors, and they are very hard to unlearn. This can interfere with empathy. Thus, early emotional triggers in the adult may lead to misinterpretations of what, in the child's mind, leads to a particular behavior. This can be resolved by returning to further self-reflecting. Then empathy can resume.

What does understanding your child's mind have to do with empathy? Understanding your child's mind is part of empathy—understanding the emotional states of another person. For example, parents form an idea of what their child might be feeling when they see a particular emotional expression on his face. It's like trying to step into your child's shoes and see from his or her point of view.

Understanding your child's mind in this way is a creative act. However, it is an act of imagination with severe limitations: no one can know another person's mind with complete accuracy. Thus, it is best to approach the task by asking questions rather than by making statements.

This empathic approach can be difficult if you did not have parents who modeled this skill. If you had caretakers in your life who didn't empathize with your needs and emotions and who didn't explore how people's behaviors impacted others, empathizing with your own children will most likely not come naturally. So, give yourself time to catch on to your child's feelings. It's remarkable how good it feels when you understand something new about your child. You know you've done well when your son or daughter says, "Hey, Mommy. You really get it. Thanks."

Empathic parents tend to raise empathic children. They become interested in how their parents think and feel and may be quite good listeners. As your child learns that he can look to you to understand his states of mind (intentions, feelings, beliefs), he becomes interested in understanding your states of mind. It's not that roles should be reversed where the child becomes the listener to the parents' problems, but it does mean that an empathic child will want to understand where his or her parents (and other people around them) are coming from.

In order to understand your child's mind, it helps to be a good observer. Verbal communication is only one piece of the puzzle. Watch your child's facial expressions to get an idea of what's on his or her mind. All these expressions indicate various emotions. Here are some examples described by Paul Ekman in his book, *Emotions Revealed*: a furrowed brow (worry or anger), raised eyebrows and lips in the shape of an "O" (surprise), a twitching eye (anxiety), crinkled lines at the edges of eyes (anger), glazed-over eyes (detachment), a wrinkled nose (annoyance), and pursed lips (fury). Speech, of course, helps us understand the other's mind, but silences, stiffening or relaxation of muscles, and facial expressions are also meaningful.

Because facial language is so important, parents are advised to refrain from saying, "Get that sneer off your face" or "Don't roll your eyes at me" when they are angry. This leads to the child hiding or masking expressions that are so essential to understanding what is on their minds. Even before they are verbal, young children interpret facial expressions, so while you are interpreting their expressions, your child is doing the same with yours.

Body language also indicates what's on your child's mind. Finger pointing or folded arms suggest anger. A droopy head suggests hopelessness. Foot shaking suggests nervous energy. Averting one's head or turning one's back may mean anger or avoidance. When the child suddenly stands up when you are sitting together, fury may be the cause, or standing may be the prelude to giving up and walking away. The better you know your child, the better you will be at interpreting your observations.

Sometimes we are blind to an emotion in our children that we block out in ourselves. For instance, an angry parent who blocks out hurt is blind to his or her child's hurt. Thus, parents can misperceive what they feel, thinking they feel only one emotion (anger) while truly feeling something else (hurt).

If this is true, then recognizing your child's hurt might lead to you feeling your own. If you don't know what is on your own mind—what you are thinking and feeling—you may subsequently be blocked from understanding what is on your child's mind—what he or she is thinking and feeling. You may draw erroneous conclusions and rashly punish. It's helpful if you understand that mental states are changeable, that they affect behavior, and that understanding them leads to stronger parent-child relationships.

If both mother and father are involved in their children's daily lives, the diverse interpretations of their communications make children feel listened to and understood. The mother or father don't always have to immediately catch on to what their child is trying to get across. This takes time. It is the parents' effort that matters. The children become more confident because both parents value their ideas and feelings. At the same time, parents discover their children are more capable than they knew as they learn the meanings behind their kids' behaviors.

Mothers and fathers may understand their infants', children's, and teens' minds differently by interpreting behaviors, sounds, words, gestures, facial expressions, and other body language in different ways, but what matters most is that both parents are interested in what goes on in their child's mind and how their child's mind works.

Parental Intelligence highlights the immense importance of this type of maternal and paternal involvement.

Summary of Understanding Your Child's Mind

Trying to understand your child's mind is essential for knowing who she is and how she thinks and feels. If parents want to change their child's behavior, they need to learn about his or her mental states. What is on the parent's mind affects what is on the child's mind—and vice versa. Parents who hold their child's mind in mind are more likely to have children who are self-reflective and secure. Parents who are able to think about their children's minds manage their parent-child relationships better and are more effective in resolving inevitable conflicts and arguments. Trying to understand your children's minds shows them you believe in them and teaches them to believe in themselves. Treating your children like capable human beings with well-functioning minds and good intentions builds trust.

STEP FOUR
Understanding Your Child's Development

There are developmental stages at which children master different skills, but not all children reach those stages at the same time. For example, your seven-year-old may be more adept at completing a math problem than a nine-year-old. Your thirteen-year-old may be more empathic than a sixteen-year-old. Two children in the same grade may perform differently on the same assignment. Have you noticed that when your first-born was a teen he had great problem-solving skills and a high level of frustration tolerance, while your next-in-line was pretty inflexible and had trouble handling frustration as a teen?

The age when a child reaches a certain skill level is the child's *developmental age* for that skill, regardless of the child's chronological age. When parents take into account the developmental age of their child—which reflects the stage the child has reached in mastering certain capacities— parents and children get along better.

What capacities should you look for? Notice your child's interpersonal skills: impulse control, effective communication, and empathy. Other skills include thinking or cognition. Watch for the development of individual capacities such as autonomy, identity formation, and self-reliance. You'll probably find your children aren't consistent across the board, but they have strengths and weaknesses.

The chronological age may not be the same as the developmental age for any of these capacities, and children may be at different developmental levels for different skills. When you set expectations for your children, be sure they reflect each child's developmental levels, which may fall behind or step ahead of their chronological age.

It helps to ask two questions: "What is expected at my child's stage of development?" and "How far apart is my child's chronological age from my child's developmental age?" Punishing or being critical of a child for not completing tasks expected for their chronological age creates problems that affect your relationship. Expectations that do not reflect your child's developmental age won't be met and will create acute emotional distress. This is especially true for a child with delays or disabilities that prevent him from reaching the general milestones of that age.

Once you have taken the earlier steps by stepping back, self-reflecting, and understanding your child's mind, understanding your child's developmental stage becomes essential for effective problem solving.

Mothers and fathers should also be aware of their own physical and emotional changes during their child's development that may affect their readiness to understand the stages their child is going through. Science journalist Paul Raeburn reported that some fathers underwent hormonal changes before and after their babies were born. He discovered that expectant fathers had lower testosterone and cortisol (a stress hormone) levels and detectably higher levels of estradiol, a hormone known to influence maternal behavior in women. Equally remarkable was his finding that the expectant father's bonding hormone, oxytocin, increased, preparing the man for involvement with his newborn.

I report these findings so expectant mothers know their expectant husbands, too, may be experiencing hormonal changes that affect them during and after pregnancy. Although these hormonal changes are different from what the mother-to-be is going through, knowing this helps her trust her husband to be more understanding of her experience.

These findings also help the expectant mother feel encouraged about her experience with her husband once their baby is born. She now knows that he will be prepared to help her understand their newborn's mind. If the mother knows that the father's hormonal changes prepared him for involvement with their infant, she can trust him more in understanding their baby's developmental needs, something they can learn about together.

Finally, it is crucial that both mothers and fathers understand that their distinct forms of parenting can affect their child's development. This is not a matter of gender, necessarily, but of individual characteristics. Michael E. Lamb, a developmental researcher from the University of Cambridge, reported in 2010 that parental warmth, nurturance, and closeness are linked with positive development, regardless of whether the parent involved is a mother or a father. Secure, supportive, reciprocal, sensitive relationships result in well-adjusted children. Thus, many mothers and fathers influence their child's development in similar ways.

Some fathers enjoy animating their babies and toddlers in active play that is less predictable and more disruptive than mothers, who may tend to create more repetitious, reliable patterns in picking up, holding, and feeding their infants. Thus the father's role in child development can be to assist the child in tolerating unpredictability, frustration, and physical activity. Father play may often not be with educational toys, like mother play, but with rough-and-tumble activities involving the body as well as an emphasis on exploration. French psychologist Dr. Labrell suggests this father-child interaction gives children confidence in taking risks.

However, it is important to emphasize that it is the individual characteristics of each parent—such as warmth and intimacy—that matter most rather than the parent's gender.

When I read about the rough-and-tumble and exploratory play encouraged with fathers, I am immediately reminded of the many mothers I have known who have encouraged their children to play in the woods, dance with them in the kitchen, participate in gymnastics, and climb trees in their yards. I also think of reserved fathers who tell stories to their children, read books with them on their laps, and observe nature quietly at a pond. Mothers and fathers have unique ways of relating to their children, and both relationships are helpful for optimal development. In terms of cognitive functioning, emotional control, and emotional and language development, relationship-building itself fosters development.

Here is a list of developmental goals that can be aspired to with increasing complexity as your child matures:

- Working toward high standards of behavior
- Developing morality
- Learning limits
- Tolerating frustration and disappointment
- Developing resilience and flexibility
- Cultivating empathy
- Encouraging multi-causal thinking
- Sustaining curiosity and persistence

- Becoming responsible
- Forming positive, long-lasting parent-child and friend relationships

It's important to understand both why children should learn to accept limits and tolerate hearing "no" and how parents struggle with these goals. Have you ever had the frustrating feeling that no one is listening when you say "No"? You try to speak firmly but find yourself asking a question instead of making a statement? You hear yourself asking, "Will you brush your teeth now?" when you mean to say, "Brush your teeth this minute!" Then you find yourself screaming, and your child is crying. What went wrong?

Parents often lack the confidence to make clear statements firmly, though kindly, when they are not quite sure what to expect of children. When you understand that your expectations are reasonable, you can make that firm statement, "Please brush your teeth now," and follow through. So let's look at when children can receive a "No" and give one themselves.

From early infancy, children learn that parents set limits on their behaviors. After a certain time set by the parent, a baby slowly learns to sleep more at night than during the day. Eventually, the baby sleeps through the night with naps during the day. Thus, the baby learns to adapt to the wake-sleep cycle expected in his or her culture. The baby learns that there are limits to how his needs are satisfied and that the parent can and will say "No."

By age two, the child is experimenting with some newfound autonomy, developing his or her own ability to say "No." Over time, this child develops a further understanding of others saying, "No, not now, later." This requires the ability to wait, to tolerate frustration, and to become flexible.

As the months and years progress, children develop this capacity more fully, although it fluctuates depending on their state of mind at a given moment. For example, a calm child without too many stressors can tolerate frustration more easily than a child in a high-stress family situation. However, it is more complex than focusing only on external stressors. There are internal stressors as well: a predisposition to anxiety, a sensitive temperament, and sensory processing abilities (how the child takes in sensory data visually, aurally, and kinesthetically and processes or understands it), to name just a few factors.

There is a developmental line for the ability to tolerate limits; this ability emerges and becomes stronger over time. If limits are not set for a young child, they feel too powerful and may try to control the adult. This is not good for them, because it is overwhelming to feel that your parent is not in control. When you feel self-doubt about being firm with every-day rules, remind yourself you are helping your child by giving them the security of clear expectations that organize their inner and outer world.

By adolescence, the child is developing a new sense of identity and autonomy. Limits are being tested regularly as the teenager finds his or her way to define him or herself in the world of peers and adults. The child who could tolerate limits effectively earlier in life has a less difficult time during teenage years. The child who has not mastered this capacity sufficiently struggles when faced with restrictions and rules appropriate to his age.

It is important even for the teenager to know that there are limits to how he satisfies his needs so that he doesn't feel too powerful and out of control. Reasonable rules and restrictions help the teen eventually develop an understanding about what he wants and what is expected of him. Although this may be frustrating, it is actually calming, because the teen then knows what is expected, when to do things, and how to respond. The push and pull between teen and parent at this stage helps the teen define himself. Teenagers rebel less often when they know their parents' motives are clear and positive. When adolescents know their parents have cared about them in the past and continue to do so by trying to understand their vantage points, they become good deci-sion-makers, following their own values even when surrounded by peer pressure. There is less pushback when teenagers know that their parents have concern for their welfare and well-being, and that setting limits comes out of love.

It is interesting that the parent is also learning to define him or herself as a parent at their adolescent's stage of development. Parents go through developmental passages in their parenting life along with their children that pertain to limit setting. For instance, some parents are more comfortable setting limits with babies and toddlers than tweens and teens and vice versa. Often this has to do with unresolved earlier stages of the parent's developmental life. For example, if a parent had a troubling adolescence that has not been understood, when their child reaches adolescence it may be harder for that parent to understand the changes their teen is experiencing and thus understand realistic limit setting.

For different parents at different times in their parenting life, it may be necessary to return to self-reflection before understanding what to expect of their child at specific stages of development. Then they become confident setting reasonable limits that their child accepts.

Summary of Understanding Your Child's Development

Parents who understand and nurture their child's development can more effectively evaluate what they can expect of their child. Misbehaviors become signals of a child's developmental stage or of a meaningful communication. The child is not viewed as "bad" but rather as distressed and in need of help clarifying his motivations and intentions. Rules can be devised, limits can be set, and achievements can be expected that fit the child's developmental age. Consequently, children can comprehend limits, tolerate frustration, be empathic of others, and form rich, enduring parent-child and peer relationships.

STEP FIVE
Problem Solving

The more you continue working on the first four steps, the more natural and effective they will become, getting you ready for the last step—problem solving. Interestingly, by now, the initial problem, the specific misbehavior, has become part of a set of problems to be solved over time. The immediate importance of the initial misbehavior may have lessened because it has been recognized as a symptom of more pressing issues lying underneath. These are the problems you ultimately hope to solve, together with your child, using Parental Intelligence.

The steps in this book that lead to problem solving are based on your desire to have a strong, healthy, and joyful relationship with your child. It is usually possible to repair a relationship, even if it has been ruptured in past conflicts. The capacity to repair the rupture is the key to a secure, trusting relationship. Without a good relationship, problems are rarely solved.

The steps leading from stepping back to problem solving seem linear, but you may need to go back and forth among them. This is truly significant because the earlier steps or lack thereof bear directly on the process of problem solving. If, for example, the problem solving efforts slip back into blaming by either you or your child, it is time to go back to earlier steps. If, as another example, you or your child consider the behavior at hand to be intentional oppositional behavior, authoritarianism, or a power struggle, then, again, it is important to go back to earlier steps. Or if, during problem solving, you find that you or your child's voice is tinged with sarcasm, you may be off track because a new problem may have surfaced, signaled by the sarcasm. Address that issue first, and use your new skills (e.g., understanding your child's mind) to identify what is driving your child to speak that way to you. If you find you are becoming sarcastic, angry, or more jittery and irritable than usual, use your new skills (e.g., stepping back) to reflect on potential triggers. In each of these instances, taking a break from problem solving to figure out your own and your child's reactions will be worth the effort.

While problem solving, you may realize you need to be more reflective about your view of reality and your child's view of reality. If, indeed, you and your child can see the problem from each other's points of view, both you and your child should be ready to problem solve together.

Let's think more about points of view. It is worth revisiting self-reflecting at this point. Maybe you suddenly realize that your child's view of an experience is similar to one you held as a child, too. This sudden realization gives you pause and helps you better understand both your child and yourself. You also realize that you were resistant to understanding your child in the first place because your child provoked the past in you, something you did not want to remember. Re-experiencing past emotions and events can have the benefit of allowing you to rethink the present event. You can then better understand where your child is coming from and solve the problem together.

Sometimes the problem that needs to be addressed isn't an event or misbehavior, but instead is the way you communicate with your child. When you realize your reactions came from the past, your interactions become increasingly empathic.

In other words, for problem solving to become possible and effective, you need to try to understand what is on both your mind and your child's mind. You need to view the situation not only from your point of view but also from your child's vantage point. If you can do so and share your understanding with your child, your child will be prompted to reciprocate. If you can't comprehend and picture your child's reality, you can't solve a problem with him.

Your child, too, needs to try to understand your view of the problem. If both of you can't embrace the other's point of view of the problem, you both must sort that out before advancing to solving the problem at hand.

Problem solving also needs to take into account your child's developmental stage, which allows you to understand your child's actual capabilities and skill set relevant to the problem.

Communication through speech, gestures, and facial expressions are affected by moods and temperaments. We all know how variable moods can be from moment to moment or day to day. Communication is not always smooth when problem solving; it can be awkward and uncertain. If you and your child expect there may be many uncomfortable moments, they won't deter you from continuing to pursue the step of problem solving.

Problem solving aims to find mutual meanings, which may be new to both participants. Meanings are exchanged through taking collaborative turns in talking things out in order to correct misinterpretations of the behavior in question.

The benefits are numerous. Both parents and children are more effective as they repair their differences and develop a positive feeling about their relationship. Parent and child learn new coping skills that can be used in the future, which fosters optimism for future interactions.

Problem solving takes time. Sticking with it and being persistent can be difficult. Also, like any plan, it's only a good one if it is carried out. Remember that it took a long time for the problems to build up; it will also take time to repair them. The challenge is to hold on to your belief that the relationship can be salvaged and the problems can be resolved. Without this commitment, things can fall apart quickly. When your child sees that your commitment is loving and genuine, he or she will feel deeply cared for and persist as well. When both you and your child are determined to use your energy to make problem solving work, it is highly likely that things will work out to everyone's benefit.

The structure of the family has been changing in recent decades. For example, current trends suggest that both mothers and fathers feel conflicted about time spent away from family and struggle to maintain balance between working outside the home, often very long hours, and spending time with their children. Although either or both parents work outside the home, they spend more time with their children than parents did in the past. This gives mothers and fathers more opportunities to be devoted to carrying out the step of problem solving with their children.

For children, problem solving is a developmental process and skill. Reciprocal interactions drive interpersonal development. When you, as the parent, engage in this process, you will find you are developing a collaborative relationship with your child. The ability to do this will rest on the mother-child and father-child relationships that have been growing as you accomplished the earlier steps of Parental Intelligence.

During problem solving, you will engage in a give-and-take between you and your child. Problem solving is a relational process. When children learn that their parents realize the underlying problems behind the original misbehavior, they become more open than ever to hearing what their parents have to say because they are feeling understood. Children are relieved to know their mother or father is open to their points of view, wants to hear about their feelings, and is aware of the developmental struggles they may be going through. In turn, as a mother or father feels the reciprocity of the open dialogue with their child, they slowly relax and trust the open, honest, and empathic communication.

In the best possible world, each parent uses Parental Intelligence and is open to reciprocal communication. If not, problem solving will be most productive only with the parent who has followed the prior steps fully.

Summary of Problem Solving

Problem solving may appear to be the single most important step. To problem solve well, however, the earlier steps are just as, if not more, important because without these steps, you may not know what the most essential problems really are.

Parental Intelligence is a relationship-based approach to rearing children as opposed to solving problems by punishment. Parents don't lose their say about their children's behaviors, but rather they understand the reasons behind the behavior, its context, and workable approaches that help their children and themselves to change the behavior or their view of the behavior.

Parents and children alike feel comfortable enough to bring their agendas to the table in the hopes of not only solving the immediate situation, but also being understood. The parents' purpose is not only to find the underlying meaning in the particular behavior, but also to help the child learn to be aware of feelings, engage in logical thinking, face challenging developmental passages, and include the art of discussion in relationships. As parents step back, reflect, understand their own and their children's minds, and learn about child development, the meaning behind misbehaviors becomes clearer, and the actual overarching problems can be solved. In a secure relationship, where parents and children engage each other in reciprocal ways, and where the concerns of both parent and child are taken into consideration, alternate means to solving problems arise.

In an insecure attachment, where the bonds are more tenuous, the work is much more difficult, since parent and child do not reciprocally engage or trust each other. Children may expect that their parents will not be sensitive to their emotional and social cues, and those children will not want to engage in discussions for that very reason. Parents may likewise expect that children will just turn them off and not want to engage in discussions. Therapeutic help may be needed to redress this distrust and shift the relationship into a more secure position.

When it is time to problem solve, children and parents may slip into avoidance tactics. They may change the subject, move around, begin a round of keeping secrets, hide their feelings about the relationship, and generally find ways to interrupt the interaction. This is where empathy comes in. Parents may need to clearly point out that their children are avoiding the discussion and they hope to understand why.

Similarly, the misbehavior that began this process may reappear, demonstrating that the parents may have begun to unintentionally avoid the problems that underlie the unwanted behavior. Parents also need to take into account that young children don't think or articulate as quickly as adults, and adults, therefore, need to allow for pauses and silences. Parents need to stop themselves from slipping into lectures and coaching before the child has a chance to absorb what is being discussed and let the child have his or her say.

Adolescents, too, need to avoid lecturing their parents with broad "philosophies of life" that drive the conversation from the issues at hand.

In time, if parent and child engage with each other, focus on their relationships, empathize with each other, and especially if parents make it a priority to identify the meanings behind their child's behaviors, a new quality of interaction will come to life, and problems can and will be solved to mutual satisfaction.

SUMMARY
Five Steps to Parental Intelligence

Through the evolving process of unlocking Parental Intelligence, each parent learns a great deal about their own mind and the mind of their child. That is, each parent accepts the challenge of learning what is going on inside himself if he is to discover what is going on inside his child. Ruptures in the relationship cannot be avoided, but the continued experience of repair secures and strengthens the relationship. The child learns to trust the parent because she believes her parent is invested in understanding a vast array of emotions. Respect and trust are earned as pleasures are shared and problems are solved.

Different parents will have found some of the steps harder or easier to master, depending on the degree of empathy they already embraced as part of themselves before beginning the process. Each reader who has come along this journey has learned how to decipher meaning behind child behavior, only to find that there are overarching problems to be unmasked.

Becoming a meaning-maker is a profound experience that can change how a parent views infants, children, teens, and, most fundamentally, oneself. Parents who have unlocked their Parental Intelligence are introspective mothers and fathers who have become willing to under-stand and take a look at themselves in order to understand their children and know how they think. Parents learn not only what they and their children think about, but also how they carry out the thinking process.

Unlocking Parental Intelligence is a new stage of a mother's or father's parenting life that will have lifelong results in how family members engage each other, care for each other, and view and solve problems over the long haul.

Let's turn to eight compelling stories of courageous mothers and fathers who live in households from different backgrounds. We will watch how these parents envision unwanted behaviors as opportunities to get to know their infants, children, and adolescents as they carry out the five steps of Parental Intelligence.

PART TWO

STORIES OF
PARENTAL INTELLIGENCE
IN PRACTICE

Chapter Four

At-Risk Parents Misread Infant's Fussy Behavior

Lara's First Months

Nineteen-year-olds Claudia and Cole married quickly when they learned that Claudia was pregnant. They had been dating exclusively for three years. One year out of high school, they were both working, and Claudia was attending a local community college. Although it had been in the back of their minds that someday they would get married, they hadn't discussed it prior to the pregnancy. In fact, neither thought they would want children. Both their parents had emotional problems, and so Claudia and Cole didn't think they would know how to raise children well. However, when the pregnancy surprised them, they had the most heartfelt conversation of their relationship and decided that having the baby was the right decision for them. They moved into a small two-bedroom apartment in a low-income area and set up house.

Claudia's mother was anxiety-ridden and suffered frequent panic attacks. Claudia's volatile father left his family when Claudia was thirteen, visiting only randomly. During elementary school, she helped take care of the house when a series of housekeepers came and went due to the turmoil they encountered. She was a chatty, giving child who tried to be what her mother needed her to be. By the time she was sixteen, she held a part-time job at Starbucks while attending high school with average grades. She was smart and could have done better, but having to work and help her mother left little time for studying. She was very responsible, though disorganized, but she barely managed to keep her life in order because she was pulled in so many different directions. Her mother loved her but was often self-absorbed and erratic. Claudia met Cole in her junior year of high school and he gave her the emotional support she lacked. By the time they graduated, they were devoted to each other. Claudia wanted to become a businesswoman, hoping that, with her years of experience at Starbucks, she could become a manager someday. After graduation, she continued working, now full-time, and took business courses at a local college. She was very energetic and diligent in her endeavors. However, when she found out she was pregnant, she was thrown emotionally.

Cole's parents had been adolescents, barely fifteen when he was conceived, and split up before he was born, so he was raised by his maternal grandparents and his mother. His father finished high school and then moved away, not participating in raising Cole at all. Cole loved his grandparents, and now, at age nineteen, he was beginning to appreciate his mother—at age thirty-four, she was finally getting her life together. In a rather romantic and dreamy way, Cole felt Claudia was his soul mate. He appreciated her loyalty and believed that, with hard work, they could make it as a married couple. He had seen his grandparents work out many problems and stay together, and he wanted to follow their example.

Claudia's pregnancy was uneventful. Her strong, five-foot-eight, athletic build supported her pregnancy easily, and Cole, a six-foot body builder, was more than capable and willing to dote on her. They consulted an obstetrician, who guided them through the process and recommended that they read up on pregnancy as the trimesters passed. Physically, Claudia was doing very well, but emotionally, she was unraveling.

By the third trimester, when the baby could be clearly seen on Claudia's sonogram, the pregnancy with a baby girl was beginning to feel real. Claudia's mother surprised them with baby clothes and furniture for the baby's room when Claudia was in her seventh month.

The much-appreciated gesture made it impossible to deny the reality of future parenthood any longer. The baby's room was chaotic: boxes of clothes and toys were piled in the crib, baskets of diapers filled the corners, and Claudia's laundry was scattered about. While Claudia and Cole had handled the pregnancy well, they had put off making plans for taking care of the baby. Claudia's business classes were over for the term, and she wasn't going to school over the summer. Starbucks was giving Claudia eight weeks' maternity leave, and Cole's boss at a deli agreed to give him two weeks' leave. That was the extent of their planning.

One night, Claudia was feeling scared, uncomfortable, and enormous, and said that she didn't really want the baby, although she wasn't going to change her mind about their decision. When her sobbing slowed, she timidly asked if they could choose the name Lara because she liked a pretty actress with that name. She knew that wasn't the best way to choose a name, but she didn't want to give the name more thought than that. Cole agreed immediately; he had not given the baby's name even that much thought, and he wanted to console his wife. Cole's grandmother was going to help the first week after Lara was born, but there was no room for her to sleep over. While this gave Claudia and Cole a bit of reassurance, these two teenagers were having a baby at a time when they clearly still needed parenting themselves.

After a rush to the hospital in the middle of the night and only two hours of labor, Lara was delivered at a healthy nine pounds, six ounces. Holding her in the delivery room with Cole by her side, Claudia felt somewhat dazed and disoriented. The nurse gave the baby to Cole, who was a bit more composed, in that he held the newborn gently and firmly, but he was visibly relieved when the nurse took her back. The nurse confirmed the couple's choice that they would be bottle-feeding and that Lara would stay in the nursery and be brought to Claudia's room for feeding and changing.

Unbeknownst to Claudia and Cole, a very sensitive maternity nurse witnessed the detachment and disorientation of the adolescent mother and talked with the head nurse on duty, letting her know that Claudia seemed to need a lot of preparation before she'd leave the hospital a day later. The nurse then spoke with a social worker, who was going to meet with the couple to discuss their plans for baby care.

By the time Claudia, Cole, and Lara arrived home, they were equipped with the name of a retired maternity nurse who would care for Lara at a modest rate when they went back to work. Cole's grandmother, waiting for them in their apartment, had organized the baby's room and filled several small bottles with formula.

STEP ONE
Stepping Back

When infant Lara was in the hospital nursery, the nurses enjoyed this easy baby who seemed cherubic due to her significant size and readiness to take a few ounces of milk at a time. She slept easily and even gained a little weight, unlike most infants who lose weight at the very start. However, once at home, Claudia and Cole seemed to be caring for a different infant. Lara cried ceaselessly unless she had a bottle in her mouth. Claudia felt rundown and sleep-deprived, and was unable to settle her baby. Cole couldn't contribute any advice, although he did take turns feeding Lara. Cole's grandmother, easily frustrated, only came to help the first few days and recommended that they call the retired maternity nurse. Claudia's mother came through and offered to pay for four months of the nurse's wages.

Claudia and her infant influenced each other. The baby's cries and Claudia's anxiety seemed to feed upon each other. When trying to put her to sleep, Claudia rocked her frantically; when trying to feed her, she pushed the nipple of the bottle into Lara's mouth; and she kept telling her to quiet down in a commanding tone. Lara was gaining weight by her six-week checkup but only sleeping for two hours at a time. Cole was back at work, his grandmother no longer came to visit—citing one excuse after another—and Claudia was frightened and alone. Months before, Claudia had felt confident; she had just been promoted to assistant manager and received good grades at college. Now that self-confident young woman was gone. She felt lost and inadequate as a parent. Feeling like a terrible mother, Claudia put off calling the caretaker, afraid that a woman with such impressive credentials would judge her harshly. Finally, two weeks before she had to go back to work, Claudia called. Unable to calm down fussy Lara, she felt she was moving from one crisis to another. Lidia agreed to come the next day, responding to the urgency in Claudia's voice warning her that she had a very difficult baby who cried all the time.

Lidia appeared promptly the next morning, cheerfully ignoring the disheveled young mother's appearance and her disorganized household. Piles of laundry, overflowing baskets of garbage, dishes in the sink, and infant toys scattered about didn't ruffle her. She instantly observed a strained and exhausted teenage mother who was unprepared for her maternal role. She noted immediately that Claudia fed her baby without looking into her eyes and that she talked to her as if she was a young child, not an infant. Lidia knew at once that she had two babies to care for and was sensitive to their anxious bonding. She noticed that Claudia carried her baby around almost all the time, suggesting how much they both needed to feel held.

Not wanting to undermine Claudia's confidence further, Lidia didn't take over and become the "better mother." But when Claudia left her alone with Lara, Lidia noticed that the baby was easily soothed with quiet, soft tones of voice. She recognized that when Claudia didn't feel able to give relief to her baby emotionally, she rushed to give her an object, the bottle or pacifier, instead of herself. When Claudia returned to the room, Lidia engaged Claudia in gentle conversation while Lara began to fuss.

"Claudia, do you think we could step back for a moment and not go for the bottle? Let's just watch Lara for a bit and think about what she needs."

"If I don't give her the bottle right away," Claudia said, "she will cry much louder and then more and more and almost never stop!"

Just the suggestion to slow down her pace was difficult for Claudia to handle, and she became anxious and distressed.

"It seems that way at first," Lidia continued in her easy, reassuring way, "but I noticed that when you spoke, she looked at you. She follows your voice with her eyes. Try talking to her, and you will see what I mean."

Claudia was hesitant.

"Okay, but . . . Lara, how are you doing? Why are you crying so much?"

"She's looking at you," Lidia pointed out. "She's been hearing your voice regularly while you were pregnant with her, so she recognizes it."

"Really? That's amazing!" Claudia exclaimed, momentarily forgetting her worries.

"Continue talking, but this time, do so in a voice that kind of goes up and down."

Claudia grimaced. "Like the funny way you talk to her?"

"Yes. I know it sounds kind of funny, but babies like it. Give it a try."

Bashfully, Claudia talked to her infant imitating Lidia's maternal rhythmic sing-song, and Lara began to coo a tiny bit. Claudia smiled tentatively and looked at her baby. She was such a mystery. Heart pounding, Claudia picked her up, and Lara was quiet. It was the first time in weeks that the two had some peace together. Lidia left the room, feeling that stepping back had helped Claudia begin to see Lara as more than a fussy baby. Lidia was sure that, in time, Claudia would learn that Lara's cries could be calls for attention, closeness, and communication, not just for feeding and sucking. Lidia was sure that Claudia was more than willing to learn and had the potential to become a comforting mother once her own worries diminished. Claudia would discover that babies could be talked to and that meaning could be ascribed to their sounds. However, Lidia knew that this development was only possible if she comforted Claudia first so Claudia could relax and comfort Lara.

STEP TWO
Self-Reflecting

A few weeks passed, and Lara was in her third month. Claudia had many more peaceful times with her infant and had tentatively begun to feel she might come to like her. With this in mind, Claudia went back to work, but she decided to take the semester off from college so she could have time to spend with Lara in her first months. She worked from eight to three without a lunch break so she could put in a full day and still be home to spend part of the afternoon with Lara. Lidia stayed until six, giving them time to tend to Lara together.

Claudia had become very emotional during these early months. At the end of one long workweek, she readily poured her feelings out to Lidia:

"Lidia, I know you said that Lara follows my voice, but I feel she prefers yours. When she hears you, she makes those cooing and gurgling sounds, but she cries with me. When I give her a bottle right away, she stops crying, but I'm beginning to catch on that it's not what she wants all the time. Even in the middle of the night when you're not here, she sometimes turns her head away from the bottle."

Claudia's reaction was typical for many mothers with a nanny or caretaker who fear that their baby favors the caretaker. But Lidia wondered if, perhaps, there was more to Claudia's feelings than that.

"Oh, so you've noticed her head turning? Good for you. She's telling you something, and you're trying to understand. So, what do you think she may want?" Lidia asked, trying to encourage Claudia to expand her way of thinking about her infant.

"I think she doesn't want me!" Claudia burst out. "I call Cole. He holds her and starts humming with his low voice, and she settles down. Then I hold her and she stops crying, but she isn't hungry. I can tell she's tired, but she isn't ready to fall back to sleep. She's just one big puzzle to me. I never really know what I'm doing."

Exasperated, Claudia sighed and teared up. Lara, who had been sleeping in her crib, stirred and started cooing. Lidia and Claudia went into her room, where Lidia invited Claudia to just watch her daughter. Claudia observed Lara intently. "She just seems to enjoy playing with her hands. See, she wakes up and doesn't even want me."

"Well, first, let's think back to what you said before," Lidia said. "She settles down when she hears Cole's deep voice humming and then quiets down further when you take her back. Sounds to me like hearing Cole's humming settled her, and then she wanted you to cradle her just like you did. She needed to feel close to your body, not be fed or changed or anything else. She knows what it feels like specifically in your arms and woke up missing that."

"But that doesn't always happen when I hold her. She makes this very contorted face and scrunches up her eyes," Claudia said trying to absorb Lidia's logic. "Sometimes, I feel kind of shaky when I hold her, and she cries. That's when she still feels like a stranger."

"Yes. You're onto something for sure. She can sense when you feel anxious, and it unsettles her. You respond to each other."

Lidia waited to see if Claudia could tolerate knowing that her anxiety could make her baby distressed.

Claudia's face turned white in fear. "So, when I'm anxious, she can feel that in me? In my shaky body?"

Lidia knew that Claudia needed to learn how to modulate her anxiety and be reassured that her infant could calm down, too. "That's right. But when you're aware of it, if you slow down your breathing and sit quietly with her, you will both calm down and feel comforted."

The color returned to Claudia's face; she was in deep thought. Fortunately, Claudia was a verbal and open young woman who readily held on to and responded to Lidia's words and warmth.

"Whoa. That feels so familiar. When I was little, like five or six, and my mother was having panic attacks, I felt very nervous and would cry. Some of the housekeepers felt bad for me and hugged me. But as soon as I would begin to get used to that and start settling down, they would leave, probably because they couldn't take my mother's ups and downs.

I don't want to be like my mother. Lara needs me to be calm so she can be. Is that right?"

"You got it. Sometimes you get anxious because you have difficulty reading Lara's sounds and movements. It is a puzzle, and it's hard to guess what her sounds and gestures mean. Like now, when she is playing with her hands and feet and looking up at her mobile, you thought it meant she didn't want you. But actually, she woke up happy and is exploring her little world. She's learning. Her behavior doesn't mean she doesn't want you; it just means she's having a good time by herself, figuring out her body and the sights and sounds around her. You have a curious little baby, which is great. You can be proud of her."

"That's amazing. Good for you, Lara!" Claudia said and grinned, feeling it meant her baby was smart.

"So let's think a bit more about why you have the tendency to feel unwanted," Lidia said.

Claudia's face became intent again as her forehead wrinkled and her eyes squinted. "Well, when I was young, I thought all those housekeepers didn't want me. It was the only conclusion I could draw when they would leave. And my mother was always leaving the room or telling me to leave when she had her panic attacks. I didn't understand it. Didn't anyone think I needed to be taken care of? I kept believing I was doing something wrong, but I didn't know what that was. As a little girl, it was very confusing, and I had no one to ask what was happening. It seemed like things kept changing so quickly. I guess I was a pretty lonely, scared kid. I was kind of ashamed of my house and never had anyone over to visit."

Lydia asked Claudia if she could see those upsetting situations any other way. Claudia was tentative and uncertain, but she was a clever girl, capable of insight. "Looking back," Claudia said, "I can sort of see they all had their own worries that weren't my fault, but it didn't feel like that then. Maybe that has something to do with it."

"Listen carefully, Claudia," Lidia said. "I think you imagine Lara doesn't want you when she is just exploring because you believed your mother and the housekeepers didn't want you when they weren't attending to you. You are confusing the past with your mother and the present with your infant. Does that make sense to you?"

Claudia, head down, said, "I really have to do a lot of thinking about that. The words sound right, but it feels confusing."

With Lidia's help, Claudia went on a path of self-reflection, beginning to contemplate how her life in the past was influencing her interpretations of her relationship with her baby in the present. Feeling vulnerable, she began interpreting her baby's behavior the way she had interpreted her mother's and housekeepers' behaviors when she was a child. At the time, she interpreted their actions only in terms of herself. Now, as an older adolescent, she had become capable of seeing things from another person's point of view, but she temporarily lost that ability when she was anxious and stressed by her new responsibilities as a mother. With Lidia's guidance, Claudia was beginning to see her baby as a real person she could get to know: a unique baby with her own specific needs and points of view.

STEP THREE
Understanding Your Child's Mind

Infants understand and see better than most mothers imagine. In her book *Talking to Babies: Healing with Words on a Maternity Ward*, Myriam Szejer, MD, notes how babies mimic their mother's smiling or grim face. Both mother and baby register each other's facial expressions and voices as a way to get to know each other.

It was evident that Claudia was primarily identifying her baby by her cries, her vocalizations of need or distress, and by the contorted grimace of her little distressed face. Through Lidia's guidance, Claudia was beginning to picture her baby as more than an amorphous moving body. A good part of the time, Lara was becoming a particular baby, one that Claudia could recognize as her very own, even though that baby could sometimes still feel like a mysterious stranger.

Lidia was trying to help Claudia realize that her baby had a mind all her own that was expressing different needs. At first, Claudia thought that babies only needed to be fed, so she reached for the bottle continually. If that failed, she thought the baby needed sucking and grabbed the pacifier. Even though Claudia didn't know how to read her baby's behavior very well, she had caught on to the fact that it always had meaning. How to soothe Lara was still a puzzle for Claudia, until she realized that sometimes just holding her baby close or talking in gentle tones was all it took. This was a revelation to Claudia. Lidia explained that it was not only the warmth and particular way she held and spoke to Lara that was soothing to the baby, but that Lara's mind recognized her mother by her smell, which comforted her. Lara's little nose was a filter for her mind that told her who her mother was.

One of Lidia's first observations had been that Claudia didn't look at her infant when she fed her. Thus, Claudia was missing out on one of the primary ways of getting in touch with her baby's mind: her gaze. Eye contact creates a primary exchange between mother and baby.

Lidia helped Claudia become aware of this. Lidia gently put a pillow behind Claudia's back as she held Lara in her arms feeding her. "Are you comfortable?"

"Yes. Thank you. You take such good care of me." Claudia smiled at Lidia, somewhat embarrassed.

"Well," Lidia went on, "when I help you feel cared for, it's easier for you to help Lara feel cared for. While you feed her, look into her eyes and tell me what you see."

"She stares at me! It's a little freaky, actually, like she is going to swallow me up with her eyes."

"Yes," Lidia said, "it's startling to you how much she wants to be a part of you. She's holding on to you with her eyes. Maybe you look away because it's so intense to be wanted that much."

Claudia sighed with some relief. "Oh. I didn't know that's what was happening. Of course, she's so little and can't do much for herself. But it's hard to be needed so much. Maybe that's why Cole's grandmother didn't stay long at all to help me and wanted me to call you so quickly. I was kind of mad at her for that, though I didn't say so. Cole told me that she said that she's been a mother twice now, for his mother and him, and wasn't ready for a third round."

"Mothering is a very big job; it brings out many feelings. I'm sure you were very disappointed when Cole's grandmother left. But you're a fast learner, and you're getting to know Lara. In fact, it might help to know that Lara has a mind of her own, and the more you get to know what she intends and needs, the easier it will be to take care of her. Oh, look! She is pulling her head back, releasing the nipple of the bottle, and beginning to look around. So what could be on her mind now?"

Lidia was purposefully drawing Claudia's attention to every detail of her baby's behavior so she could become a good observer, too, and begin to be creative in understanding what each movement of her baby meant.

"I guess she's saying she's finished with the bottle for now and interested in something else."

Claudia moved Lara out of the feeding position in her arms and laid her on the couch, so she could look up at the rattle she'd been shaking. Lara cooed and smiled.

"Smiling is the coolest thing ever. This past month, I've begun to see her smile more and more. I guess that means she is happy. Thank goodness. I told Cole last night I never thought I could have a happy baby."

Although Cole wasn't part of the picture during the day, when he came home after Lidia left each evening, Claudia told him everything that happened in the afternoon. Lately, Claudia had more happy details to report, which eased his worries while he took part in feeding Lara and holding her.

STEP FOUR
Understanding Your Child's Development

It is in the physical intimacy with sucking, swallowing, smelling, holding, and hearing the mother's voice that a baby begins to create herself. In his *Collected Papers: Through Pediatrics to Psycho-Analysis* (1958), Donald Winnicott, pediatrician and psychoanalyst, states that there is no such thing as a baby without a mother. That is, when we see a baby, we see her with her mother; they are part of a whole. This concept is the essence of an infant's development. Claudia seemed to sense this, recognizing at some level how important she was to her baby, although she couldn't have put it into words at that time. That was precisely what made her so anxious: her responsibility as a mother was tremendous. Without a good example of being mothered in a soothing way, she had a lot to learn.

Thus, Lidia was playing an integral role in Claudia's passage into motherhood. She was with her when Lara started to smile more and more often in her third month and even began to laugh. Lara cooed, saying "oh" and "ah" as she gazed at her mother, which enchanted Claudia. Lidia reminded Claudia that Lara's sleep schedule was becoming more routine as she slept for six hours at a time at night, giving Claudia more rest. She pointed out how Lara liked to lie on her tummy and lift her head to look around, as well as lie on her back and enjoy lights and mobiles above her head. Lidia also showed Claudia how Lara followed everyone with her eyes and reached for objects—exciting milestones.

By the end of the third month, Claudia and Cole had heard Lara squeal with delight, continue to follow objects with her eyes, and even bring her hands together. One night, to their surprise, they saw her roll over in one direction. Because Lidia pointed out all these details to Claudia, she, in turn, came to enjoy pointing them out to Cole. They had become very conscious of their daughter's development and were enjoying it. In turn, Lara felt the joy that her parents felt toward her, which gave her a positive image of herself as someone who was wanted—a feeling Claudia had missed all her life but was beginning to know about herself, as well. Her husband and her baby wanted her, and she knew it securely for the first time.

STEP FIVE
Problem Solving

During her fourth month, Lara was able to sit up without support and hold on to a toy. Cole and Claudia found that she resisted giving up the toy when it was time to move her to another room for feeding or sleeping. Claudia and Cole argued about what to do about this behavior. Cole thought it didn't matter and she could bring the toy with her, but Claudia insisted that she had to learn to listen or she would become a spoiled baby. Claudia remembered that when Lidia first came to their home, she had thought Lara was a "difficult baby" because she never seemed to stop crying. But she had subsequently learned that she just didn't understand the meanings of her cries and that, in fact, Lara wasn't difficult at all. When Claudia learned there were many possible meanings behind the crying—and thus many ways to ease Lara's complaints—she learned that what seemed like fussing and crying was communication. She didn't want to make the same mistake again when Lara held on to the toy, although she was beginning to think that maybe if she didn't address it, Lara could become a "troublemaker."

When parents are problem solving, it's often important to go back through earlier steps to gain a full understanding of the behavior in question. Claudia had learned to step back with the "fussing" problem, so it seemed natural to do so again, although she would need many repetitions of this process to internalize it fully. When she stepped back, she observed that Lara often picked up objects, held on to them awhile, and then put them down, exchanging them for something else. Claudia realized it was a kind of playing. She noticed that Lara was quite intent and good at it. When she and Cole discussed it, Cole thought that if she was holding on to something tightly, that he could exchange another toy with her and enter the play. So one night when it was time for sleep and she was holding a hard rattle, he took the rattle and exchanged it for a stuffed animal she could keep with her while sleeping, and she stopped protesting instantly. Cole was very pleased, but Claudia still had doubts. She was impressed with Cole's ingenuity but decided to discuss it with Lidia the next day.

Claudia's insight that Lara was "playing" was very significant. Play is an essential developmental step. When a baby plays by herself, it increases her sense of self and creativity. When playing with another person, interpersonal skills develop. It is an enriching activity that leads to complex ways of thinking and relating to others. Cole naturally entered the play by exchanging different objects with Lara. He was expanding her curiosity and exploration of new objects, as well as deepening their mutual, enjoyable contact. Claudia needed to find out whether what she feared might be a potential problem was actually a healthy and essential development.

Claudia told Lidia about the behavior. Claudia cleverly analyzed that the meaning behind Lara's behavior was her desire to learn to hold things and let go of them, but she still felt strongly that if it was taken from her gently and she was told to let go, she should listen. Otherwise, she would always want "her way" when she was older.

Lidia agreed with Claudia's first view of the meaning behind Lara's behavior and pointed out that meanings of behavior change with age. She praised Claudia for being so attuned to Lara's needs and emphasized that if Claudia not only watched her play but also played along, this interaction would enhance their closeness. That way, Claudia added pleasure and fun to the positive things she was giving her daughter.

Lidia clarified that this was also true for Cole's play with Lara: the purpose of the activity was mutuality, and they were getting to know each other better. When she was older and understood more language, listening and following directions would be something to learn, but she wasn't old enough for that yet. Lidia clarified that Claudia thought there was a problem in part because she was thinking of Lara as an older child, not as a baby.

"Why is this so important to you?" Lidia asked. "Lara is such a good baby, don't you think? Why are you worried she won't listen to you when she's older? She isn't a troublemaker now."

Claudia was quiet and pensive. "Now that you ask, I think it goes back to what we talked about before, when I felt I was the cause of my mother's anxiety and the stream of housekeepers leaving. When my mother was having panic attacks, she would scream at me to leave the room, no matter what I was doing. I felt bad, like . . . a troublemaker! When she gets anxious now and slips back into that frame of mind, even as an adult, I still have the feeling I did something to cause it."

"So," Lidia asked, "what's the connection with Lara? Think hard, because this could come up again and again."

Claudia breathed deeply, and tears came to her eyes. "This isn't easy. I think I'm mixing what I see in myself with what I see in Lara. I don't want her to become what I thought I was."

"You said you don't want Lara to become what you thought you were," Lidia responded gently. "You weren't actually a troublemaker at all. You were a little girl with an anxious mother who wasn't thinking clearly when she shooed you forcefully out of her room. She did it so often that it's deep inside of you, and you have trouble remembering that she was making a mistake in the midst of her distress."

Claudia cried. Wiping her eyes after several minutes, she hugged Lidia, who held her close.

"Being a mother makes you relive being a child," Lidia continued. "You were not a troublemaker, and there is no reason at all to think Lara could become one. Like you said, she is just playing and doing a very good job of it. She's growing beautifully. And by understanding the meanings behind her behavior, you are helping her experiment and learn."

Claudia felt emotionally drained, but the heavy atmosphere in the room had lifted. She felt relieved that Lidia was helping her because it was only in getting to know herself that she could get to know Lara. Lara was awakening from her nap, cooing and smiling. She always woke up refreshed and happy.

Maybe I'm learning to be a good mother, Claudia thought.

The next day, Claudia saw Lara holding on to a toy: a long yellow rattle that made noise when a ball inside its circular end made a clacking sound as it hit the circle over and over. Lara squealed happily. Claudia got on the floor with her to join in her play and talked to her in a lively manner about how much fun she was having. Claudia seemed to naturally sense not to dominate the play, but to follow Lara's lead. When Lara let the rattle go, Claudia picked it up and shook it heartily, making the clacking sound. Lara laughed robustly, and Claudia laughed, too. Claudia was responsive and sensitive. Mother and daughter were shaping each other as they learned to enjoy each other. Lara was free to express herself openly and was understood by her mother, who was learning to love her.

Chapter Five

A Distressed Child, Not a Bad Child

Two-Year-Old Ted

Ted Daver, a two-year-old adoptee, lived with his parents in a warm, luxurious one-story home along a river in Portland, Oregon. A wiry and lively fellow, he would play happily for long stretches of time in his elaborate playroom filled with shelves of children's books, racing cars, work trucks, a large train set, and a basket full of balls. But his deep-set blue eyes, which shone under his long, dark bangs, revealed a serious demeanor. Sometimes his mother would find him lying on their heather-colored couch staring up through the skylight in their living room at white wintery skies. Other times, she found him sitting crouched over on his bed in his cozy, blue-painted room filled with stuffed animals and warm blankets knitted by his paternal grandmother, sobbing inconsolably. At only two years old, Ted already had a complicated history preceding and following his birth and displayed behavior that was difficult for his parents to handle. Eventually, his mother found a weekend seminar on Parental Intelligence because she and her husband became invested in the process of finding meaning in Ted's behavior.

For the first nine years of their marriage, Ted's highly educated parents assumed that they would not have children, but when Mrs. Daver reached thirty-nine, she began to wonder if she had made a mistake. Because she could not get pregnant, she suggested adoption. She was a beautifully groomed, stunning woman, a successful financial analyst who enjoyed a full social life and travelled extensively with her husband. Underneath her polished, forthright exterior was a warm, gentle woman with growing maternal instincts. Her husband—a tall, olive-skinned, imposing, successful entrepreneur in a high-tech company—was less enthusiastic about having a child, especially if he couldn't be the biological father. He liked their childless life and didn't want to change it. As their discussions progressed, however, he began to see his wife's softer side emerge; he respected her changing priorities and wanted to get to know this new side of his companion. She touched something inside of him that he had kept under wraps for a long time. Because he loved her, he consented.

After several months of research into adoption and multiple interviews by adoption agencies, Mr. and Mrs. Daver were accepted for a domestic adoption. Eight months later, they adopted Ted at birth. Although there were no clear complications, the social worker mentioned that the biological mother had been distraught when she was separated from her child. Although she had originally requested not to hold the baby after his birth, she asked for him after all, held him for two hours, and even fed him twice.

The birth mother wanted to remain anonymous, and so the Davers knew only the essentials: She was a healthy, intelligent, single woman in her midtwenties who worked for the US government, traveling extensively to high-stress crisis situations around the globe. When she became pregnant, she knew her lifestyle wasn't suitable for a baby. She thought her infant would find a better home with others who could provide well for him. She had good prenatal care with regular obstetric visits. A lawyer and the adoption agency had arranged that the Davers and the birth mother would not meet, and that the infant would be given to them after he had spent a day being monitored in the hospital nursery. The unforeseen change of the birth mother's attitude and the time she spent with the baby unsettled the Davers, but Ted went into Mrs. Daver's arms with ease and, except for the excitement and joy they felt, their trip home was uneventful.

After four months of tender loving care, Ted's mother hired a nanny and returned to work. At first, Ted had difficulty adjusting to his mother's absence. The well-trained and highly experienced nanny reported that although Ted cried like normal babies, he also made weeping sounds. She felt that although he was gaining weight properly, he drank in fits and starts, as if he was having trouble feeling content. His parents received advice from their pediatrician on how to help him adjust, and over time, due primarily to the nanny's highly attuned soothing ways, he adapted. He learned to tolerate his parents' daily absences and came to love his playful, sensitive nanny.

However, by the time Ted was eight months old, his father began to silently resent the decision to adopt Ted. He found himself staying at work longer and falling asleep earlier, leaving his baby's care to his wife. Their social life was curbed. They saw their childless friends less frequently and no longer went on the vacations they were used to. For Mr. Daver, life had changed too significantly. He hated to think he didn't love his son, but he didn't find much pleasure when he was with him. His wife, who enjoyed making their stately home into a child-proof house with toddler clutter—toys, diaper bags, an indoor baby swing—seemed to be changing more than he could have foretold. Husband and wife grew distant.

When Ted was a year and a half, his father broached the topic of divorce. This wasn't the life he wanted. Although he didn't voice this out loud, he also wasn't sure this was the wife he wanted. Ted's mother was beside herself, and endless hours of talk ensued. For six months, they discussed a possible separation without taking any action.

Then a crisis hit. Ted had just turned two when the nanny announced she had to leave. The nanny had formed a close bond to Ted in the twenty months she had cared for him, so this was a shock. Luckily, Mrs. Daver quickly found a small daycare center with excellent references that seemed like a nurturing place. Two adults cared for only four children on the ground floor of one of the caretaker's split-level home nearby. It seemed ideal.

Ted's mother adjusted her schedule and arranged with the daycare providers that they'd continue keeping the notebook used with the nanny, where Mrs. Daver would note details about Ted's morning before he arrived at daycare and one of the women would note details about his day for Ted's mother to read when she picked him up. This had been very helpful in the past, keeping her abreast of his daily life while she worked, and it would prepare the caretakers each day as well.

During the first week of daycare, Ted began to have temper tantrums. The first occurred when his mother tried leaving the first morning. Ted screamed and cried, stomping his feet, throwing toys, and hitting one caregiver. Mrs. Daver left after half an hour, troubled knowing he was still crying and flailing about. At the end of the first week, the caretaker told her Ted was having tantrums three or four times a day. The notebook was filled with examples of his meltdowns. They seemed to occur during transitions between activities, for instance, from playing to napping or from napping to eating. Then they seemed more random and began to last longer. While at first they lasted up to fifteen minutes, they soon progressed to half an hour or even more. The caregiver described how Ted refused to be comforted with hugs, making his body rigid and immobile with his arms clasped around himself. His tantrums were so extreme that his screams caused the other children to cry.

When Ted's mother came to pick him up, he ignored her. The caretaker explained that he was likely mad at his mother for leaving him in the morning. Ted's mother tried to understand, but she felt rejected nonetheless.

Soon the tantrums happened at home, and his father resorted to punishment. He put Ted in his room alone for ten minutes and closed the door. When Mrs. Daver peeked in, the expression on his face as he sat immobile on his bed told her Ted was shocked and scared. She learned he didn't know why this was done, even though his father said it was because he was "bad" for making such a "fuss." Ted fell apart. His tantrums turned into mournful sobbing.

Even so, every time Ted had a tantrum, his father placed him in his room for ten minutes. It didn't help; in fact, Ted's behavior got worse. Screaming, sobbing, banging on his door, his emotions whirled out of control. His worried mother pleaded with her husband to make the punishments two minutes, not ten. But this didn't work either. Ted and his parents felt entirely helpless.

Around this time, Mrs. Daver read about the Parental Intelligence Saturday seminars in her local paper. The seminar would take place on five consecutive Saturdays. The article described that parents would learn to find the meaning behind their child's behavior in five steps practiced at the five meetings. Desperate, Mrs. Daver convinced her husband to participate. They recruited his mother to watch Ted and off they went, anxiously anticipating what lay in store. The seminar was limited to eight parents, so they felt they would have a chance to talk about Ted.

STEP ONE
Stepping Back

Mr. and Mrs. Daver had a complicated marriage that was falling apart, and as it did, two-year-old Ted was falling apart as well. So, what were the unacknowledged reasons for Ted's tantrums?

His parents knew from other experiences in their lives that sometimes it was best to step back and take stock of a situation before proceeding. So, they readily followed the first step toward Parental Intelligence. They were told to roll back the clock to review their memories like a video in their mind to the last few years, not just to the last tantrum.

During lunch break at the seminar, Mr. and Mrs. Daver sat by themselves and talked intently. They recalled going to the hospital to meet

Ted. Mrs. Daver wondered if Ted's contact with his birth mother had an impact on him. She worried about how he had developed as a fetus and what his life was like in utero. Ted's father had never entertained the idea that a fetus responded to his environment or that a newborn had feelings. To him, an infant was more like a vessel that needed to be filled and emptied, not a living being with a mind filled with emotions.

Overwhelmed by anxiety, their minds and ensuing discussion jumped from the hospital to his first few weeks at home. Despite all their preparations for their baby, Ted's needs encompassed their days much more than they had imagined. Mrs. Daver did most of the feeding, changing, and soothing, while Mr. Daver barely looked on. This was a very foreign experience for him, and he was tentative and cautious around both Ted and his wife. He confessed he was relieved to go back to work after two weeks, letting his wife take over. In contrast, she said she began to gain confidence as a parent in those weeks. She was emotionally ready and deeply involved; he was not.

This discussion was all they could handle at lunch, and they didn't talk again until that evening after they had put Ted to sleep. He had a good, tantrum-free day with his grandma. Mr. Daver, already affected by the seminar's goal of finding meaning behind behavior, found that interesting. What did his mother do that he and his wife were unable to do?

During the week, Mr. and Mrs. Daver continued stepping back, talking in the evenings. They had taken to heart what was said in the seminar and continued valiantly on their own. They remembered how the nanny became a significant person in all their lives because she made their days run smoothly and she and Ted formed a close attachment. Mrs. Daver told her husband that she silenced her feelings as she shifted back into her work life. She put all her trust into the nanny, who, she rationalized, was a better mother than she could have ever been. She had felt Ted was fortunate.

But then the nanny left. Mrs. Daver became very anxious remembering her unsteady feelings at the news. She asked her husband if he had noticed how frantic she felt then and what impact he thought her anxiety had on Ted. Mr. Daver said he didn't know; it all seemed like a blur. This was because he had actually remained impassive to the events, letting his wife negotiate the new waters.

They reviewed the notebook. It awakened them to the days after his nanny left. They recalled for the first time how Ted would lie on the couch for seemingly long periods of time and wondered if this was meaningful. At the time, they concluded that he was not getting enough sleep but hadn't questioned why. He had always been a good sleeper when the nanny was around. Now they wondered if he'd actually had a sleep problem that followed her leaving, and they queried further if he couldn't sleep because he was sad, longing for her. Stepping back to recall these events led them to ask themselves if they were so overcome with what was happening after she left that they only hoped to make the difficulties go away by rushing Ted into daycare without asking, "Is there meaning to all this?"

Mrs. Daver was surprised during that first week after the seminar to find her husband reading the notebook on his own. Once, she couldn't help but watch his serious demeanor when he didn't know she was looking on. She felt a bit secretive and intrusive, but seeing his wrinkled brow and head in hand, she couldn't walk away. It hit her hard because she knew something inside of him was changing. The notebook had taken on a life of its own.

When they continued to consult the notebook together, in their minds, they started to create a sequence of Ted's life after the nanny left. When Ted entered daycare, he began to have tantrums when his mother left him in the morning.

As this was still going on, Mrs. Daver told her husband how worried she felt:

"I have to force myself to leave to get to work on time. Then I keep interrupting my work with thoughts of how to handle my leave-taking. When I go back to pick him up, I feel hurt that Ted avoids me and doesn't run up to me to give me a hug. I get so overwhelmed by my own feelings that I can't grasp what Ted is going through."

Mr. Daver tried to be reassuring. "I didn't know what a struggle this has been for you. You're such a good mother. Ted loves you. What happens next? How do you get him in the car?"

"His caretaker told me to wait for Ted to come to me instead of pursuing him. She pointed out that Ted had his own emotional pace and that it would help him if I respected it and would wait for him to be ready. Ted takes his time, but slowly comes to me. Today, after three days of this, he gave me a long hug. When I felt his body against mine, we both relaxed and felt relief."

When Mrs. Daver described these experiences to her husband, he took on that worried demeanor she had seen in his study when he was reading the notebook. He held her while she cried. Sharing these feelings seemed to bring them closer for the first time in months.

I was so oblivious to what she was going through, he thought. *She and Ted have something together I am not a part of. Do I want to be?*

Mrs. Daver made an appointment and met with the caretakers while Mr. Daver stayed at home with Ted. He watched Ted with uncertainty as he played with his favorite toy trains quietly and by himself. The scene felt surreal. He was so outside the emotional plane of his child, he felt fear sweep over him. Stepping back had helped him see his vulnerable son with a clarity he had not let in for two whole years.

Stepping back had also helped Ted's mother. It opened her to a new recognition, with the caretakers' help, of the broad spectrum of feelings Ted may have been experiencing. She had previously thought his tantrums were unruly, bad behavior, and she was at fault as a parent who didn't know how to discipline him. She didn't know what she was doing wrong. She had not considered until now that the tantrums were a complex expression of a deeper meaning.

By suspending their judgment about his behavior, both parents suddenly recalled Ted standing at their bedroom door one day as they talked about the possibility of Mr. Daver's leaving the house. They realized they were so embroiled in their conversation that they didn't consider postponing their argument. They recalled that they weren't even wondering what Ted understood. Ted's speech was very good—in fact, it was exceptional for a two-year-old—and his comprehension was even better. They previously assumed he knew nothing of the potential divorce. But by stepping back, they began to consider that Ted may have known much more than they assumed. He had heard their arguments and quiet discussions for months when the nanny had gone home at night and he was alone with them. The nanny wasn't there to ensure he was in another room where he couldn't hear his parents' discussions. Precisely what he understood wasn't clear, but he at least began to sense that his parents weren't getting along, which made him feel insecure. His father was talking about "leaving" the home, and it was safe to assume that hearing the word "leaving" was having a significant impact on him.

The Davers' thinking had opened up considerably by going back in time to find clues to Ted's present unhappiness. This was a change in their parenting mindset. They asked themselves how these changes that multiplied in Ted's young life could have influenced his meltdowns. Rolling back the clock brought all of this to light in deepening, heart-rending impressions of their son's emotional world.

STEP TWO
Self-Reflecting

The second Saturday seminar seemed to arrive very quickly. The Davers rapidly grasped the presenter's explanation that in order to understand Ted's mind, they first needed to understand their own minds. They were learning that they needed to account for their active and passive responses to their son's behaviors.

In the safe confines of the parent group, they began to benefit from reflecting both separately and together on themselves as parents. While listening to the others, Mrs. Daver thought to herself: *What was happening to us during the difficult struggles in our marriage that led us to ignore the changes in Ted's life?*

Tentatively at first, Ted's mother timidly shared her blind spots during her son's first two years: "I think our marital troubles blocked me from thinking about what Ted was going through. I remember my hopes and dreams for a baby as we went through the arduous adoption process. So why did I continue to work such long hours when a baby had been such a priority? My work partner, a single mother, asked if we both could consider working part-time from home. But I felt so invested in our long-term clients, I didn't even consider the idea."

Mr. Daver was more reserved. He kept his thoughts to himself. He was trying to figure out why he was feeling so removed from his wife, even though he became a father out of love for her. *Why was I a man who did not want children?* he wondered.

Other parents in the group acknowledged that only if they understood themselves could they possibly consider what was happening to their child. The Davers agreed. They realized that as they were weathering transitions in their own lives, they had not seen the impact of these transitions on Ted.

In order to proceed, the moderator suggested that sometimes changes and losses in parents' lives when growing up can make them blind to the changes their children are enduring. Mrs. Daver grabbed her husband's hand and revealed that her mother died when she was thirteen. She described being in shock by its suddenness. Unfortunately, her father grieved alone, and no one seemed to realize that a thirteen-year-old needed help mourning the loss of her mother. Vivid details from that time came to the surface swiftly.

"I continued with my daily school schedule and got increasingly quiet, withdrawing into a shell. I got some solace from a teacher, but it wasn't sufficient to make up for the lack of care from my father. He was so self-absorbed."

The presenter pointed out that this was a second parental loss. She gently conjectured that having to bury her unresolved pain may have blinded Mrs. Daver to Ted's pain. To think of his needs meant to relive her experiences.

Mrs. Daver had an "aha" moment: "When I came to pick him up at daycare after missing him and he avoided me, I was reliving the feelings of my father avoiding me after my mother died." These feelings were very deep, and bringing them to the surface churned up painful melancholy.

Mrs. Daver now understood how Ted's actions made her feel so rejected that she couldn't see that his tantrums were emphatic calls for help. She felt he was doing something to hurt her, not to reach her, and when she wasn't there for him the way he needed, he just escalated his behavior, trying even harder to get the attention and care he needed from her.

Mr. Daver listened closely to the other men describe their relationships with their fathers. As they talked, he thought about how, even before he met his wife, Mr. Daver had always been a strong, ambitious competitor with little time for close relationships. His connection with his father, Ted's grandfather, revolved around athletics and work. There was no room for feelings. His father was also a competitive, successful businessman who continued to be athletic in his older adulthood, an example Mr. Daver followed. He and his father related over ball games on television and playing basketball. Feelings were foreign to them, and they both avoided them.

Mr. Daver wasn't surprised that his wife shared such an important part of her life with the group. Since she became a mother, she was much more emotional. Before then, he realized that shared activities and long work hours had bound them together. Becoming a mother showed a new side of her. Despite his participation in the adoption, he wasn't ready for this change. He couldn't admit to the group, or even later to his wife, that he didn't want a child, so he had kept his distance, seeing his son as his wife's child. He didn't know how to be close to people—adults or children—and was unaware that children's needs could be different from his own.

Reflecting on these insights led Ted's father to wonder how he could help Ted find his way. Self-reflecting had increased his sense of responsibility for his son and his wife, and his darkening thoughts led him to realize they would have to help Ted together, challenging his view of their son being only her child. He thought of his own mother for the first time in this process. She had always rallied to his side when his father was distant. He recognized that it was her influence that gave him the courage to face having cast aside a paternal part of him: he could feel parental himself, rather than assigning that role only to his wife.

It is important to note the shift within Ted's father. This imposing, sophisticated man was finding a part of his inner self from which he had shielded himself. He was becoming a sensitive parent. Clearly, the adoption process doesn't make someone a parent. It was Ted who was making his father a parent by making himself heard. Stepping back and self-reflecting had let Ted's vigorous voice resound inside his father's mind.

That evening, Mr. Daver shared with his wife his thoughts about his limited relationship with his father that led him to worry about his limited contact with Ted. He told her that trying to punish Ted for his temper tantrums was thoughtlessly following his father's parenting style, although he had resented it when he was young. He said that he now appreciated the closer bond with his mother who fought with his father over punishment. He pointed out that a similar source of marital tension was occurring between them.

"You are very much like my mother who made our household feel like a home," he murmured. "I have to do my part now as an understanding father. I must support you and Ted with comfort and love."

He was a bright man, capable of gaining sensitivity due to the warm influences of his mother and wife. He was beginning to comprehend that parental actions in the form of even moderate punishment felt harsh to an overwhelmed child. Self-reflection was opening up a new emotional vista for him and offered the promise of a stronger relationship with Ted.

Ted's parents discussed how their marital dilemmas influenced their parenting styles. Because their commitment to their marriage had become tenuous, their capacity to unite to discuss their son's needs had been limited. Self-reflecting about their past experiences had led them to get to know each other better and care more about each other's feelings. They felt their marriage was entering a new phase. They appreciated each other's struggles as children who grew up in families where emotions were not taken into account.

They decided to invite Mr. Daver's mother to be more involved in their family life. She spoke often of wanting to spend more time with Ted. They hadn't followed through with her before because they were so caught up in their work lives and embarrassed by Ted's behavior. Now they realized she was a loving resource who would help them, not judge them.

STEP THREE
Understanding Your Child's Mind

Prior to self-reflecting, Ted's parents hadn't considered that their two-year-old son had a mind of his own and that for two years he had been processing very stressful situations. When the topic of understanding your child's mind came up at the seminar, they poured out what they thought were their multiple sins about not understanding a long list of stressors on Ted's young mind.

They went back and forth telling the group what happened in a frantic torrent of words: the loss of his birth mother—Mrs. Daver going back to work—the nanny's arrival and departure—the shift to small group daycare. The presenter tried to interrupt to ease their anxiety, but Mr. Daver couldn't hold back his self-reproach for how he threatened to leave home. The Davers saw the tears in the other parents' eyes as condemnations, but they soon learned that their story was causing the others to feel guilty about how their own decisions had stressed their children. Their tears were expressions of empathy and care. The eight parents were forging a nurturing bond as their stories resonated with each other.

The presenter pointed out that it was natural to feel self-reproach for imperfect lives, but they could put their feelings to better use by thinking about their child's mind, which harbored thoughts, feelings, intentions, and needs of his own.

When the Davers were alone, they discussed Ted's internal world as a baby. Mrs. Daver had read about a fetus's experience in utero. She knew that when Ted unexpectedly spent time with his biological mother right after birth, he would recognize her voice and temperament that he had grown accustomed to in utero. Mrs. Daver worried that after being with his birth mother for a while and leaving her permanently, the abrupt shift to Mrs. Daver's arms might have jostled his mind. As the adoptive mother, her voice was suddenly strange and novel. Her husband reassured her that her voice and comforting quickly took over and continued day and night.

When Ted's tantrums began, Mr. Daver didn't realize that his little son's mind was filled with loss and grief; he only thought his son was attempting to get his way, though he didn't know why. After so much thought, Ted's father began to see the pain and fear on Ted's face during his tantrums as an indication of what was in his mind. He recognized that putting Ted alone in his room to punish him was the wrong choice because he felt shut out from his parents like he had felt from his nanny and possibly from his birth mother. Mr. Daver applauded his wife for demonstrating that she was in touch with Ted's mind when she asked him to shorten the punishments. She was thinking about what Ted's mind could tolerate.

He looked at his wife intently and spoke quietly and emotionally: "I now see that when I sent Ted to his room, he also might have felt like I just left him again like I do every morning when I go to work without so much as a 'good-bye, see you later.' And then, he overheard all the conversations about my leaving home entirely! How can I forgive myself?"

He shuddered. "It never occurred to me before that I had any effect on his mind. I was so closed off from him. I guess because I never want to feel like I depend on anyone, I didn't understand that he depends on me. I've let him down. And, sweetheart, I've let you down, too. I'm deeply sorry." He was crying.

After their talk, Mr. Daver was motivated to do some research. He told his wife that according to Annie Murphy Paul's book *Origins* (2010), the stressors a pregnant woman is living through affect the fetus.

"It startles me to realize that Ted was probably in a very high-stress intrauterine environment while his pregnant mother was traveling from one threatening part of the world to another. She likely experienced difficult and dangerous situations and reacted with extreme caution and vigilance. Paul talks of the risk of transmission of such reactions from a pregnant mother to her baby, who experiences them after birth. This would mean that Ted could have heightened sensitivity and vigilance to changes. We need to observe him in the future to see if he is overly cautious or watchful."

Because he was becoming better informed about how Ted might experience change, Mr. Daver felt he was becoming a better parent.

They now understood why Ted fell apart. His temper tantrums were mini-breakdowns caused by cumulative losses. They were also attempts to communicate that he needed help containing his emotions. They felt a sense of renewal as parents who understood their child's mind and could now respond to him with more wisdom and love.

STEP FOUR
Understanding Your Child's Development

Mr. and Mrs. Daver got a book on early child development to prepare for their next seminar. They found that Ted had reached the milestones of a two-year-old. He used symbolic play—when a child uses figures and toys to represent important aspects of his life and to create stories. They decided to pay more attention to the stories he made up as clues to what was on his mind. He also showed motor planning skills, such as walking downstairs to eat breakfast, brushing his teeth, and getting dressed. He demonstrated a sense of causality: if he greeted his mother with a smile, he saw she smiled back. He was developing fine motor coordination by building with small blocks and gross motor coordination by running and jumping.

Ted's vocabulary was comparatively large, and he was able to articulate his routine wants and needs and allow a parent to say no to him when appropriate. He had the beginnings of a moral sense of right and wrong and could play alongside other children. While the nanny was in his home, Ted slept well throughout the night and could soothe himself to sleep if he awakened.

In the seminar, the presenter pointed out that this development was a testament to his good care because his cognitive and motor development had not been compromised, despite the losses he sustained. His mother's bodily warmth, voice, gestures, and characteristic patterns of feeding and soothing gave him the emotional bond he needed in order to grow.

According to Trevarthen and Condon in *Before Speech: The Beginning of Interpersonal Communication,* infants engage in prespeech by four months, which includes mouthing speech sounds of the mother accompanied by gestures made by the baby's limbs that pick up the rhythm of her speech. Hence, by four months, Ted was fully involved with turn-taking interactions with his mother on a daily basis that were then broadened with the nanny. His reaction to the abrupt change from his mother to the nanny during the day was communicated by Ted's weeping sounds and short bursts of sucking the nanny observed. However, he did eventually adjust to this highly attuned caregiver and appeared to her to be functioning well during the day before she left. Unbeknownst to the nanny, Ted was witnessing his parents quarreling in the evenings.

By one and a half, Ted had far fewer words than he would have six months later; however, his listening comprehension exceeded his verbal vocabulary, so when his father started talking about leaving home, he heard that his daddy was talking about going away, though he didn't understand why, and his struggles escalated. With his heightened watch-fulness, he probably followed his mother's intense gaze at his father while he was speaking in strained and sometimes raised tones. He also observed the distressed expressions on both their faces in the months they talked about separation. Surely, this was disturbing.

The discussion in the seminar helped the Davers put together the many facets of Ted's first two years. They figured out that his emotional development was ultimately stalled when the nanny left. The nanny's departure was a finality that he could not comprehend and reverberated viscerally with the final break with his birth mother. The loss of this first attachment was embedded in his mind as a template for future attach-ments that, unfortunately, repeated in unexpected losses he was not prepared for.

By the time he entered daycare, his grief was full blown. There was increased separation anxiety when his mother left him with the care-takers, and Ted began expressing his grief through tantrums. Because his parents did not understand that these cumulative events were losses, they did not know to create transition periods from one caretaker to another, which would have supported his emotional development. For example, Ted's adoptive mother could have stayed at home with the nanny for a few weeks as he got to know this new caregiver. Then, sim-ilarly, his mother could have spent time in the daycare center until Ted adjusted to those new caretakers. They now knew they needed to sup-port his emotional development during any future separations with such careful planning.

His inability to control himself at two was the clue to the cumulative pain he'd been suffering. Tolerating this much frustration, disappoint-ment, and unexplained loss was far beyond his young years and important not to underestimate.

According to Inge Bretherton in *Children's Theories of Mind: Mental States and Social Understanding*, during the second year, language assumes a more significant role in communication and interchange with others; however, meaning is still primarily expressed through intentional gestures and actions, such as Ted's laying on the couch for extended periods of time, his difficulty sleeping after his nanny left, and his temper tantrums after entering the daycare setting. Bretherton points out that by about nine months, infants expect shared understanding. That is, they expect that the meaning of their utterances and body actions are shared by their listeners. This illusion was prematurely shattered for Ted when he found out that he wasn't being understood, even when he escalated his efforts to express himself.

STEP FIVE
Problem Solving

Ted's parents had undergone a great deal of reflection and learning about their child's mind and his development that helped them build a keen sense of Parental Intelligence. It represented a great deal of emotional work and growth. After so much time understanding his mind and development, problem solving came naturally. Now that the Davers grasped Ted's complicated psychological picture, they could address his uneven development: his cognitive, language, and motor development was soaring while his emotional development was lagging far behind. They decided he needed to be with them more with greater continuity.

Because his language was growing, his mother thought she'd try to talk about feelings with him. At first, she didn't directly address feelings of loss and separation anxiety but just gave him a feeling vocabulary with his play people. She made up stories about what made a little boy figure happy and sad. She found a girl doll and said she was happy because her daddy was hugging her. Ted started to use the words happy and sad for himself. This little bit of feeling vocabulary started showing up at the caretakers'. One caretaker called home and said that Ted was saying, "sad, sad" when he saw another child cry. When he was having fun painting, he said, "The boy in the picture is happy." The caretaker encouraged Ted's mother to keep up this feeling talk in play as she would at the daycare center.

Then, one day, when Ted was crying as his mother was leaving the center, she hugged him and said, "Ted, are you sad that Mommy is going to work?" Ted held on to her tightly then went off to play. All he needed was that moment of perceptive recognition and acceptance of what was on his mind to enable him to let go of her and join the others. Ted's mother felt so relieved and hopeful that they could relate at that level. Ted knew his tears were understood.

Ted's father had a harder time with feeling language because he barely used it himself. However, watching his wife with his son opened a new emotional portal for him. When he got home from work one day, he asked Ted if he wanted to play. This was the first time he'd ever paid direct attention to him as soon as he walked in the door after work. Ted immediately took him to his toy trains and showed his father how they went around the track. His father noticed how Ted looked up at him with delightful anticipation. Ted's father didn't know much about train play, but he eyed the basket full of balls. He knew about ball playing. Smiling, he told Ted, "Hold your hands together like a bowl and see if the ball can land in them."

At first, Ted dropped the ball, but after a few tries he caught on: "Daddy, I did it!" he exclaimed. They were enjoying each other. Lightness and excitement were in the air.

Mr. Daver was engaging with Ted in activities he knew well: sports. He never realized before he could actually play with a two-year-old. To his amazement, he felt wanted himself, which was a new kind of accomplishment.

Ted's father went on the Internet to look for a gym for tots. He discovered what was called a soft gym, a place with a multilevel large structure of slides, tunnels, an enclosed space with netting with hundreds of soft balls to jump in, and a cushioned floor. It was advertised for two- to four-year-olds. He told his wife about it, who was clearly surprised by his initiative and interest, and they all took a trip to the gym one Saturday. While Mrs. Daver watched, Ted and his father jumped and climbed and slid down very long slides. The flooring was soft and bouncy, so there was no chance of getting hurt. Ted spontaneously began to follow a four-year-old girl and got very brave. Whatever she did, he followed. He was laughing heartily, having a wonderful time. His father was having a great time, too. His little son was not afraid of this new, very physical experience. In fact, he loved it. Mr. Daver was proud of him. Following the four-year-old added to the fun; Ted even gave her a hug, which astonished the little girl and tickled Ted's dad. Finally, after two hours of play, Ted was tired out. His elated mother fed him, and he fell asleep in his stroller. Mrs. Daver told her husband how impressed she was with his ingenuity and the pleasure he found in his son. Mr. Daver admitted he never would have done all this if they hadn't experienced the temper tantrums and gained the Parental Intelligence to understand them. He told his tearful wife how he felt such profound affection for Ted and, indeed, for her.

Ted's parents had a lot to work out between them, but they had begun problem solving at a level Ted could participate in. Ted had brought out their compassion for him. The tantrums dwindled and stopped on their own. Once the Davers understood the tantrums were just Ted's way of communicating his emotional struggles, they responded with the continuity and care that he needed, the deeper problem that they needed to solve. Ted's mother and father felt a deeper love and respect for each other, and talk of separation stopped. They had grown as marital partners and as parents.

Further, because Mrs. Daver felt that Ted needed more continuous care from her, she decided to follow her colleague's suggestion about working from home. Looking back, she laughed at herself for so quickly rejecting the notion when she knew nothing about what was in store for her as a mother. Now, as the senior partner, she was ready to make new work decisions, so she could build upon what she had learned about how much maternal care her son needed from her. Their company had been successful for over ten years with a steady group of clients. They could stagger their days in the office if each woman spent two days each week working half days at home, taking the rest of the days off with their children. Energetic, Mrs. Daver planned on getting up two hours before Ted awoke in the morning and spending two more hours working during his nap. She took the weekend and Monday and Tuesday at home, so he had four consecutive days with her and three days at daycare. She made a calendar with pictures, so he could understand when he would be with her and when he would be at daycare. She prepared him each evening for what to expect the next day. She also spent as much time as he needed to ease his transition, waiting until she was sure he was happily playing at the daycare center before she left. When she returned, he rushed to her, taking her hand to lead her to see all that he had done that day. His emotional development was blossoming.

Ted's parents' Parental Intelligence had reached a significant height that would continue to develop as they and Ted grew. The gateway to becoming a tender, loving family had been opened. However, this was just the beginning of how raising Ted was reshaping who they were and who they could become.

Chapter Six

A Boy with Asperger's Can't Stop Singing

Four-Year-Old Lee

Carl and Deirdre Wolf lived in a comfortable, two-story home in the heart of Columbus, Ohio, with their three sons. Vic was a tall, well-built, vibrant ten-year-old who had his father's dark eyes and bushy eyebrows. Eight-year-old Wade was a heftier child with blond hair like his mother and a more serious temperament than his older brother. He worked hard at everything he did with meticulous care and follow-through. Then there was the little one: animated, chatty four-year-old Lee who had his mother's fine blond hair and small features and a more solitary spirit. By age four, he was growing like a weed, seemed more awkward physically than the other two, and was developing a striking vocabulary and an outstanding memory for numerous facts that interested him. Lee was the completion of the family picture Carl and Deirdre had planned.

When the couple decided to have three children, psychologically-minded, warm, and sensitive social worker Carl chose to interrupt his career to be a stay-at-home father while his talented wife, Deirdre, decided to continue to build her architectural practice. They had a passionate marriage, as they complemented, admired, and loved each other.

Carl was a rather private person; he enjoyed staying at home tending to his children and working in his studio as a sculptor of birds made from wood. The boys were accustomed to playing with their chosen activities by his side, sometimes learning to use tools with their father. Before the children were born, Carl enjoyed homemaking more than Deirdre did and was accustomed to cooking, doing laundry, and carrying out other household chores. So, unlike many stay-at-home fathers, he didn't find baby, child, and home care overwhelming. He was fairly active in a meetup group sponsored by the national At-Home Dad Network, where he found other like-minded fathers.

During Carl's first two years with Vic, he took a seminar on Parental Intelligence and took to its approach quite naturally. When Wade was born, he reviewed his learning materials and notes and continued along the same path. His personal philosophy was that children were individuals whose needs and sense of identity should be respected. When Vic had just turned three, a neighbor asked him if he was like his mommy or like his daddy, and Vic responded swiftly, "I'm me: Vic." Carl felt he was succeeding.

As the boys grew, Carl made a conscious decision that he was not going to get pressured into the "new wave of scheduled socialization" middle-class parents in his community seemed to ride on, organizing multiple activities for their children to give them a competitive athletic and intellectual edge. He felt these children were overscheduled by their helicopter parents, and although many of them adapted to this structured lifestyle, he felt they weren't given a chance to naturally explore and discover their interests and talents while socializing with others in a more random, natural way. He feared that if he followed the tack of his neighbors, his kids might find it hard to learn how to organize time on their own and experience pleasure by themselves and with others.

When Vic or Wade expressed a particular interest, Carl booked the lessons and organized the activities they chose. He strongly believed that each boy was different and would flourish at his own pace and in his own ways. Wade chose Suzuki violin lessons. Carl, who had no musical talent, was in awe of his son's talent and enjoyed being a part of it. He never had to urge Wade to practice for his lessons—this was what he wanted. Vic was a gifted ice hockey player, both rugged and graceful, and a great offensive strategist, but when he was pressured by his coach to join the traveling team, he declined, preferring to spend his weekends at home. Carl supported both boys' instincts, feeling very proud and pleased.

Carl was particularly attuned to his children as infants and toddlers, in part because of his social work training. He was a sensitive observer of their eye, hand, feet, and body movements and always found great pleasure in noticing small changes. By the time Lee was eight months old, Carl noticed that his facial expressions were less animated than he remembered from his other sons. While, as infants, Vic and Wade sometimes turned their heads to the side when Carl's broad grinning face became too intrusive, Lee seemed to turn away more often. Much of the time, Lee seemed neither happy nor unhappy. Carl was becoming aware that Lee exhibited an interpersonal indifference. At times, he felt snubbed as a father who had been used to laughing and hanging out with his sons. However, he respected Lee's wishes when he preferred to be left alone.

When Lee was one year old, Carl realized that Lee didn't enjoy being touched as much as the other boys, and he had to hold back his usual affection and roughhousing. Lee crawled in a timely manner but walked a little late, at fourteen months. Carl recognized that, even for a toddler, he had an awkward gait. It didn't worry him; it fit his belief that the boys would have their individual characteristics. Sometimes he felt Lee was too uninterested in him as his father, but that, too, he chalked up to "kids are different."

Carl was determined to allow Lee to be his own person and develop in his own way. Although Lee didn't begin saying single words until he was fourteen months—later than his brothers—it made sense to Carl that he started naming things at the same time he started walking because his words seemed to develop as his environment was growing. By two, he was speaking in short phrases, and by three, he was a chatterbox, especially about things that interested him, which also made sense to Carl.

Vic and Wade began complaining about Lee when he was about three-and-a-half. They said that Lee only wanted to talk and not listen: he wouldn't actually carry on a conversation, and he didn't look at them very much. Carl told them to give him time, although he confided to Deirdre that Lee did go on talking much more than anyone would want to listen, didn't care if anyone responded, and seemed to be developing an unusually advanced vocabulary pertinent only to his favorite interests, such as toy cars. He lined them up endlessly in exactly the same way each time and counted them over and over. He knew minute details about each one and loved to talk about them repeatedly.

When Wade would try to join in four-year-old Lee's play and just touch a car or move it in another direction, Lee would get intensely distressed. He would jump up from the floor and start flapping his arms. Wade would become distraught watching this and put the car right back. Lee would promptly calm down and go back to lining up the cars the way he wanted. The oldest brother, Vic, was less patient. He would race the cars around the room, testing and teasing Lee's tolerance. Appearing stunned, Lee would sit and rock back and forth. Vic thought this behavior was "weird" and was frustrated with his brother, but did not want to be mean and rearranged the cars for Lee, who would promptly change the location of any cars out of his specific order.

This kind of play made it impossible for Lee to share with other children. Lee's preschool teacher recommended that Lee be evaluated. Carl and Deirdre hid their hesitation from each other, but complied. Much to their surprise, the evaluation turned up a diagnosis of Asperger Syndrome. The diagnostician explained that sharing would be difficult for Lee, and his desire to do things his specific way and remain solitary would not just evaporate with time. Carl and Deirdre learned that Asperger's was a pervasive developmental disorder characterized by problems with socialization and communication. They felt fortunate that the school had recommended an evaluation, because all too often, Asperger Syndrome was missed at such a young age. The diagnostician added that although Lee was on the high end of the autistic spectrum and would probably not have language or intellectual impairments, he had little ability to read social cues, even though he talked to people all the time—or more accurately, at people.

Even though Carl had been watching Lee's development closely, it was difficult for him to absorb this diagnosis. He didn't want to pigeon-hole his child with a classification, but he had to admit that he had been trying to rationalize Lee's behavior for some time. Deirdre, however, was beside herself. On the one hand, Lee looked and sounded so competent. On the other hand, it seemed like he would be relying on them longer than they had imagined. Together, they were slowly realizing that they had to find new ways to care for him.

One evening, the three boys were watching a funny music video that Lee enjoyed immensely. Remarkably, he memorized the theme song instantly and sang it. After the movie, at bedtime, Lee kept singing the song repeatedly. His brothers closed their doors so they wouldn't have to listen. At first, Carl and Deirdre felt proud of Lee for memorizing it so quickly, enjoyed his performance, and told him so. Deirdre coaxed Lee to brush his teeth and take a shower, two things he didn't enjoy because being clean was unimportant to him. (While lots of kids don't want to wash up before bed, for Lee it was so unimportant because of his problem with socialization.) Finally in bed, Lee continued to sing, which prompted his exhausted mother to yell, "Shut up, Lee! No night-time snack." This outburst surprised both herself and Lee.

After not seeing the boys all day, Deirdre was usually patient and attentive. But she was deeply distressed with the diagnostician's evalua-tion. Lee was astonished by his mother's reaction and cried frantically. Her yelling disturbed not only his expectations, but also his hypersen-sitivity to sound, which Carl had intuitively shielded him from and avoided for many months. The threat of no snack was upsetting to Lee, not because he was hungry, but because it meant losing a regular, expected routine.

Deirdre quickly reversed herself and got him a snack, which she served him with repeated apologies. Deirdre and Carl knew that this incident had unearthed deeper problems. They had a lot to face.

―――――――――

STEP ONE
Stepping Back

Carl and Deirdre practiced stepping back all the time. But they had not yet absorbed the very disturbing information they had just received. They were afraid to even think about it because it brought forth a lot of guilt. They had so many questions: Have we done something wrong? Are we to blame? Should we have known sooner?

At first, they realized they both thought it had been fun and even remarkable when Lee started singing. After all, he had a sweet voice and had instantly memorized a song. They felt he was performing for them, and they were his delighted audience. But as his singing continued, each admitted experiencing a growing nervous confusion. He didn't seem to notice them while singing. He wasn't looking at them for their reactions as he repeated the song countless times. Even though they were feeling increasingly uncomfortable, they didn't know that this repetition and poor eye contact was part of Asperger Syndrome.

Deirdre felt ashamed. "I felt provoked and shut out by Lee all at the same time. I work a long day and try to give him so much attention. Maybe it's unfair, but when I felt ignored, I also felt unappreciated, and I lashed out at him. I never do that, and I apologized like a crazy woman. Then I was the one who couldn't stop talking! The thing is, he couldn't help himself, and I treated him as if he could."

Carl put his comforting arms around his wife and said with regret, "I'm always so determined to let them develop in their own ways that I kept rationalizing away the unusual aspects of Lee's behavior instead of realizing that something was very wrong and he needed help. He's four now, and in retrospect, I knew something was wrong when he was three. I could kick myself! I wasted a year of his life not learning what to do for him. Maybe I should have entered into his play more, even when he seemed to want me to stop. The diagnostician made it sound like he'd never understand social cues. I won't believe that. Now I'm determined to find out how to not mold him, but stretch his capacity to socialize. I refuse to believe it can't be done."

Deirdre responded quickly and kindly. "Oh, Carl," she said. "We mustn't blame ourselves. It will only hold us back. We must reflect on our feelings if we want to help Lee. You are the boys' captain, the leader of the troop, their outstanding father. Please don't forget that. We will find ways to support our lovely little boy, too."

Parenting had always seemed pleasurable to Carl and Deirdre, even exciting as they learned from their children's interests and personalities, but now, hiding despair as they tried to buoy each other up, they weren't so sure.

STEP TWO
Self-Reflecting

Carl and Deirdre began sharing how they each learned to make friends and socialize—normal childhood trials—so they could get a handle on how interpersonal relations developed. Their parents weren't big social-ites, and neither were they. Still, each had friends individually and as a couple. Their general congeniality seemed to rub off on both Vic and Wade, who had made friends on their own without much help from them as parents. Together, they reflected upon how social interactions were mysteries to Lee.

Deirdre recalled how hard it was for her to join social groups as a little girl. Her interests in building things and drawing intricate designs of houses started in grade school. She was quite focused at a young age and spent hours drawing and constructing creations she one day wanted to live in. She couldn't find other girls who shared this kind of fun and stayed away from girls who told secrets and appeared mean. She didn't feel she fit in, so she often stayed by herself. However, she made one best girlfriend in second grade, and they were still close now as adults.

Carl found socializing easier because he was athletic and made friends through team sports. But he also remembered being teased for being the "teacher's pet," the boy who always had the right answer in school. He took it in his stride, though, because he was an easygoing kid who enjoyed his knowledge and wasn't going to hide his striking memory. He admitted sheepishly to Deirdre that he'd liked boasting. It gave him confidence. He was an avid reader and loved collecting all kinds of facts. In that way, he realized he was like Lee. But unlike Lee, he was sensitive to other people's feelings, which was foreign to Lee. When tougher kids had bullied him, he backed down and understood how to tone down what exasperated others. Now he worried about how other kids would treat Lee, who was not in control of his idiosyncrasies.

Given Deirdre's social awkwardness, she leaned on her husband at social gatherings because he was friendly though not unusually gregarious. The couple understood each other's needs and had a close bond, looking out for each other in large social groupings. They both grew up as only children, but they had not wanted their children to grow up alone because they believed that socializing began with siblings at home. They were happy with that decision, but realized that Vic and Wade were confused by Lee's general indifference to them. They wondered if the older boys felt Lee didn't like them, or if they disliked Lee.

Both Deirdre and Carl questioned whether they had passed some genetic precursors of his problems to Lee. Carl had always desired to amass knowledge, like Lee, though Lee's interests were narrowly focused.

Socially, Carl liked being private, but he was attuned to others and didn't share Lee's solitary style, lack of social awareness, and minimal emotional relatedness.

Deirdre didn't fall into lengthy monologues like Lee, but like him, she often spoke in a flat, unexpressive voice that made them both seem as if they were insensitive to how others treated them. In truth, however, both could get hurt easily. Deirdre's face was sometimes unexpressive and often did not match how she was feeling. Carl knew to ask her how she felt or he'd misread her.

Dierdre's speech was often more formal than the situation asked for, and people had pointed that out to her. She used words such as "aforementioned," "shalt," and "henceforth" in everyday conversation, and Lee picked them up. Coming from a four-year-old, these words sounded even more peculiar. In follow-up visits with the diagnostician, Deirdre and Carl learned that children with Asperger's are more prone to model their speech patterns after adults rather than their peers.

"Come to think of it, my mother speaks that way, too, which is where I must get it from," Deirdre told Carl and the psychologist. She decided to be mindful of her word usage so she wouldn't make Lee's problems worse. Both Carl and Deirdre realized that both her parents sometimes sounded as if they were from another century.

"Maybe the genetic line to Asperger's came from my side of the family," said Deirdre, ridden with guilt. "My great uncle is legendary in my family for having been a recluse and spending all his time writing extensively on Asian history. I don't know if he wrote well in terms of a literary style; it was more like he enjoyed collecting facts. He had no interest in being with other people. No one knew where he picked up his interest because he eventually stopped talking to anyone and lived in isolation; his books are still around."

Their self-reflection on their own socialization patterns increased their sensitivity to Lee's difficulties. His inability to take turns when playing and in conversations was on top of their list of priorities for improving Lee's socialization. They agreed that, for the sake of all three of their sons, they had to learn a lot more about Asperger's.

STEP THREE
Understanding Your Child's Mind

Lee's mind affected the way he understood the world around him. Deirdre and Carl needed to take cues from specialists and from their own research to imagine the world from his perspective. Feeling understood by each other helped them feel supported as they lived with Lee and tried to understand his feelings and motivations.

First, they considered Lee's poor eye contact. It occurred to Deirdre that if Lee didn't look at others, he didn't learn about facial expressions. She knew that her face was hard to read, but Carl's was very expressive, dramatically so, which was precisely what had attracted her when they first met. Carl observed that Lee looked more easily at Deirdre than himself, which he conjectured was because her face was less stimulating. They drew a tentative conclusion that Lee could only tolerate a little stimulation at a time, so Carl tried to avoid broad expressions. Wade's more serious nature was easier for Lee to deal with than Vic's full-body gestures and hearty laughter. Carl and Deirdre felt they were catching on to what it might feel like to be inside of Lee's mind. Even the smallest stimulus could be too much.

It was apparent to Carl that Lee was sensitive to noise, even though he made a lot of his own by chattering and singing. Carl realized that Lee experienced the sounds he made himself much differently than those he heard around him. Carl concluded that other people's voices became an undifferentiated noise that reverberated strongly, creating a high level of insecurity and anxiety. Deirdre noticed he would cover his ears at dinner when everyone started talking at once. She also recalled that he instantly covered his ears when she yelled at him that one evening.

"Lee covered his ears in the grocery store this afternoon," Carl told Deirdre. "He couldn't cope with the crowds and the noise. That must have felt like chaos to him. He complained a great deal and folded himself on the bottom rack of the cart, put his head down and covered his ears."

Lee didn't seem to have a good filter. In an environment where all sounds blended into a cacophony, he couldn't focus on his father's voice as he tried to soothe him. All sounds, including his father's calm tones, competed for his attention and overwhelmed him. Lee couldn't filter out extraneous sounds in the store like the squeaky wheel on their shopping cart or the ring of the cash register. It was as if all sounds, including Carl's calm voice, competed for his attention at once.

Carl said, "The sounds in the grocery store were like a garbled, painful noise Lee couldn't get relief from. I was so glad for him when we finally exited and I quickly buckled him into the security of his seatbelt in the quiet, familiar car. I give him a lot of credit for not making a scene with so much inner turmoil," he added.

Carl and Deirdre learned that another reason for Lee's poor eye contact and downcast eyes might be a sensitivity to bright lights. Light that was normal to most people was too bright for him.

As if this wasn't enough, Carl reminded Deirdre how Lee's play was very restricted. He seemed obsessed with his cars. Lots of little boys loved their Matchbox® cars, but Lee played with them in a limited, repetitive way: he'd line them up repeatedly in always the same precise order, naming each car meticulously. He was so preoccupied with his arrangements that his brothers had begun to stay away from him. They complained that he was never interested in what they liked to do.

Vic remembered that when they were younger, Wade used to do everything he did, which was annoying sometimes because he could never play by himself. But he said, "This is much worse. He's never interested in what I do. He talks like a robot and acts like he's the only one in the room!"

Imagining a world that was too loud, too bright, and too social for Lee's coping mechanisms helped Carl and Deirdre realize how profoundly difficult it was for Lee to learn everyday social cues. His lack of social interaction meant he was far behind children his age. Add his odd mannerisms from flapping his arms and rocking his body when stressed to his odd word usage, and other kids found plenty of reasons to stay away from him, further reducing his social experiences.

"Lee seems to be communicating with his behaviors," Carl explained. "I imagine if Lee tried to put into words what he was experiencing when he did things repeatedly, he'd say something like, 'I get confused. I'm scared when things aren't as I expect. When I do it over and over, I know what's going to happen next. Don't interfere or try to stop me.'"

Carl and Deirdre were coming to grips with Lee's thinking patterns where, in order to stay calm, self-involvement overtook any tendency for exploration. The night he enjoyed the music enriched his world for a while. He had fun. He could enjoy himself with others, which was so wonderful and rare. Unfortunately, this episode ended in a mini-disaster because his singing took on a life of its own, apart from the family. He couldn't control himself when the unrelenting repetition of his song took over. Repetition had become the enjoyment. It seemed to help him control and give order to his easily overwhelmed sensory world, excluding his audience instead of feeling pleasure with them. The singing made more sense to him than the people who loved him, because people are not predictable. People don't do the same things in the same ways according to the same rules Lee could follow. The unwritten social rules other people follow were inaccessible to him because he could not interpret gestures and tones of voice.

With this deeper understanding, Carl and Deirdre felt more prepared to talk to Vic and Wade about their brother's world.

STEP FOUR
Understanding Your Child's Development

Carl and Deirdre chose a quiet night after Lee went to bed to talk to Vic and Wade about Lee's diagnosis. They gathered in the living room.

"Mommy and I wanted to talk to you about Lee," Carl began. "He's too young to understand this discussion, so we waited until he's asleep. When he's older, we will talk to him, too."

"We all love Lee very much and want to understand him," Deirdre continued. "Daddy and I know that you have noticed that Lee has some unusual difficulties. We learned that he has something called Asperger Syndrome, which affects the way he interacts with other people. He doesn't understand how to have conversations, how to take turns when people talk. That's why he talks for a long time without seeming to give each of you a chance to speak. We've learned that when he is interrupted, he just waits and continues where he left off."

Vic had a very intent expression on his face. With furrowed brow, he asked, "Is this a disease? Can he be cured? Can he take medicine?"

Carl didn't expect this question and had to pause before he answered. "It's not like he is sick with the flu, which can be treated with rest and medicine. He will struggle with his difficulties his whole life. It has to do with the way his brain makes him experience the world around him. Sometimes older kids with Asperger's take medicine to help with the way they do things over and over, but Lee is too young for that, and there are many other ways we can help him."

"It's important to understand him, not only to help him, but also because he could unintentionally hurt your feelings," Deirdre said. "He doesn't understand other people's interests, so he only talks about his own, and you may think he doesn't like you. But he does. He just doesn't understand how to show it. For example, lining up his cars over and over may seem boring to us, but it is reassuring to him. He gets upset when we try to change the order because change scares him. This is different from the way other kids play at his age. We can try to stretch his ability to play in more varied ways, but we have to do it very slowly so it doesn't scare him too much. And we all notice that Lee doesn't look at us directly very often. That, too, is because it is scary for him. People can make him nervous, even us, so he looks away—"

"I know Lee has these problems," Wade interrupted, "and I've always wondered why he was different. But I also think he's really smart."

"Yes, Wade," Carl said, smiling. "The exciting aspect of Lee's abilities is his record-breaking memory."

"Yeah. I noticed that the night Lee sang," said Wade. "I thought I was the only musician in the family until that night. He memorized the lyrics and tune in a flash. Lee likes music. That's definitely cool."

However, there were things about Lee that bothered him. "Sorry to say this about Lee," Wade went on, "but Lee doesn't take a bath or shower every day, and I don't know why you don't make him. Is that part of his problems, too?"

"Yes, it is," Carl responded. "I know he's only four, and most kids don't mind being messy, but that's not what it's about for Lee. He's not concerned about what others think about him. Because he doesn't know much about being with other people, he doesn't care at all about showers and how he looks, but I'm sure we can think of ways to change some of that." Carl knew Lee wasn't dressing himself completely every day like a typical four-year-old. To get him out the door on time, Carl was still pulling shirts over his head and putting his socks on, while Lee prattled on in his monotone monologues.

Wade had apparently noticed that, too. "You know, Dad, Lee may have this problem, but, like I said before, he definitely isn't stupid. I think he's pretty smart for a four-year-old. He knows all kinds of facts. He knows he needs underwear, a shirt, pants, socks, and shoes every morning. If you keep doing it for him, he'll never learn. I want to learn more about how his brain works differently than mine, but I don't think he should be treated like a dumb little punk."

"Does it seem unfair that he's treated differently?" Carl asked.

"Sort of," Wade admitted. "I don't exactly get it yet. I care what I look like. I want to fit in with my friends. Maybe at four it's different. But Lee wears the superhero shirts that once were mine. You bought them for me. I liked wearing them. I told Lee I liked his shirt, but he didn't give a hoot. He just walked away."

"How did you feel when he walked away?" Carl asked.

"Kind of bad. He didn't care what I said. But I'm used to it."

"It's hard to get used to," Carl said. "It was nice of you to try to tell him that you liked his shirt."

"Could you get him a shirt with a car on it so he could like his shirts, too? Like I did at his age?" Wade added softly. "He's my brother. I want him to be happy."

"I know you do, and we can try that," Deirdre responded. "Let's all do some thinking about how to help Lee and we can talk more another time. Daddy and I want to know your questions and ideas whenever you have them, and we especially care about your feelings when things happen between you and Lee."

Vic had been quiet during the discussion, but he did a lot of thinking afterwards. He knew from his own ten-year-old observations that his little brother was clumsy. His friends' four-year-old brothers were running around playing games all the time. Lee barely moved. He could accept that Lee was awkward, but he didn't have to sit on the floor with the same infuriating cars all day long. He didn't want his parents to think he wasn't kind, so he didn't say that, but when his mother said they can "stretch" Lee's ways of playing, he had some ideas.

The next day, Vic went up to his room where he discovered four of his old Matchbox® cars and a large digger truck. He sat down and stared at them, remembering how he used to play with them so differently than Lee. He'd zoom them around. He took one of the little cars that he didn't think Lee owned and went downstairs.

He went over to Lee and said quietly, "Hey, Lee, I have a surprise for you. A present. Look!"

Lee glanced up at Vic quickly and eyed the car. He said a quiet "thanks" to Vic and added the new car to his lineup.

Vic started some conversation, "Lee, how many cars do you have?"

Lee counted to twelve.

"Hey, that's a lot," Vic said, "I have more to give you. Do you want me to get them?"

"Okay," Lee said.

When Vic brought the other three to Lee, Lee gave him a smile and let Vic add the others to his long row. Vic remembered that Lee had trouble looking at him and thought Lee may feel a little nervous now when he was trying to play with him.

Vic counted them again out loud and announced to Lee, "Now you have fifteen." Vic kept his voice tone low, so Lee wouldn't get too excited and scared. "Where are all the cars going, Lee?"

At first, Lee didn't reply, but Vic waited patiently. Lee finally said, almost inaudibly, "To the store."

Vic got some blocks and put them together. "Here's the store, Lee. The car in front is going shopping." Lee let him move the car to the blocks. Then Lee quickly moved each car up to that first one, so they were all in line again.

Carl was sitting quietly in the living room while they played. He was pleased that Vic took his time with Lee. This much patience was unusual for Vic. Carl was glad Lee had been able to join Vic's play by answering his question about where the cars were going. Lee was adding a storyline from his life: going to the store. He didn't know that Lee could create a storyline. He wondered if he understood the blocks stood for the store, because by introducing a make-believe store, Vic was adding a symbolic element to Lee's play. He wasn't quite sure what Lee understood. But if he understood symbolic play, then Lee was on the right developmental track for a four-year-old, and he was pleased.

This kind of play was new for Lee. Carl felt it was a very promising step forward. He was being social by playing with Vic, and he was not just counting things, but using them, however briefly, as they were intended.

Vic was pleased. He went to give Lee a hug, and Lee quickly backed away, but he smiled and looked at Vic for a second and then looked aside. He swiftly withdrew again and turned his back to Vic. But what magic Vic had engineered! He had managed a bit of change with his brother.

Vic had entered where his father dared not go, teaching everyone a valuable lesson about child development for kids with Asperger's. Be sensitive, but never give up.

Having witnessed Vic's ability to expand Lee's play, Carl decided he should have a future discussion with his older sons about the fact that a child with Asperger's takes things literally. He recalled a time when he asked Lee, "Can you count to twenty?" and Lee answered, "Yes," but didn't count. He also recalled the time when Deirdre told Lee, "You have my eyes," which Lee countered with, "I have my own eyes."

Carl and Deirdre reflected on how their discussion with his brothers had affected the older boys' behavior and sensibilities. The couple's growing Parental Intelligence was helping all three sons.

STEP FIVE
Problem Solving

Wade was clever about getting Lee a T-shirt that pictured cars, his interest. He'd discovered a way to show Lee that others knew what he liked. This would help Lee connect with others to help with his interpersonal difficulties. Vic went even further by actually playing and interacting with Lee ever so gently and patiently, stretching his capacity to play with someone else. Due to Wade's and Vic's ingenuity, problem solving had already begun. Wade's thoughts caused his father to take a few steps toward Lee's independence. "Lee likes routines. I could use it to his advantage. Why shouldn't he lay out his clothes the night before like Vic and Wade have been doing for years? Deirdre taught them that. Lee could easily remember to do it, too, if his drawers were organized with shirts and pants that matched."

So they organized Lee's dresser to add greater order and predictability to his life. Lee's four-year-old development was very slanted toward routines that could be put in place for him, and his memory was foolproof. Put those characteristics together and you might get a shiny, clean kid dressed for preschool on time.

Capitalizing on Lee's great memory and preference for routine, Lee was told that there was a "one-two-three-four morning rule": one, brush teeth; two, wash face; three, underwear and socks; four, shirt and pants. Wade turned it into a song, and Lee joined in right away. He tended to want to just sing the song and not follow through, but the boys were also doing something together. Lee was socializing with Wade because they shared an interest—music. That, indeed, was the way to connect with Lee: through his interests.

The whole routine didn't work in one magic morning, but after two weeks, the routine was in place and Carl told Lee how proud of him he was, another positive interaction.

Further, Carl sensed Lee was proud of himself, too. He spontaneously told Lee to look in the mirror, something he had never seen Lee do. Lee looked in the mirror for a few seconds, then walked away abruptly. It was a spur-of-the-moment suggestion on Carl's part. He'd never read about a child with Asperger's doing that. But those few seconds were very encouraging to Carl. Lee was looking at his own body, some kind of recognition of himself from a little distance. This was an enormous victory for Lee, no matter how brief, because it meant he was joining the social world of people who observed themselves.

Carl told Deirdre about the moment in the mirror. She was intrigued. Another day, Deirdre asked Lee when he and Wade were both in front of the hallway mirror. "Lee, stop a sec. Look at you and Wade in the mirror. What does Wade see when he looks in the mirror?" Lee looked at Wade standing next to him for a moment, then glanced at the image of himself and Wade standing side-by-side in the mirror. Wade started laughing while Lee just stared. Lee paused, turned to see Wade grinning, and then walked away, but the question had been asked and could be asked again. Slowly, Lee might be able to grasp that people see things and think things differently than he does.

Carl had often asked himself the question, "Could Lee love?" It was hard to be in Lee's mind. He wondered, *Did he care that it was Vic in*

particular who gave him the new cars? Did he enjoy his singing in a differ-
ent way when Wade sang with him?

A few weeks later, Vic gave Lee the big digger truck. This was a brand
new experience. He took Lee outside to dig up some dirt. Lee was tentative at first, but then he became very focused on how the truck worked.
He kept digging over and over again, ignoring his brother. Vic didn't
interfere with Lee's new experience. He just sat quietly by his side. But he
felt overjoyed when he saw Lee shooting a smiling glance his way.

Expanding his environment was a huge gain for Lee, but Carl wondered if he was motivated not only by the chance to increase his car
collection at first and then add a truck, but if he was also motivated by
some curiosity about Vic. He had never been interested in Vic. In fact,
Vic was a source of anxiety because, from Lee's perspective, he was too
loud, moved too much, and provided too much stimulation. Vic was
someone to avoid. But Vic was acting out of love now that he was sensitive to playing with Lee at a slow pace, capitalizing on his interests. Could
Lee feel that Vic was reaching out to him? Did he know?

Deirdre decided to tell Lee directly about Vic's feelings for him,
adding a vocabulary about emotions to his repertoire of words. What
prompted her wasn't only her desire to maximize his language development but also to add an interpersonal component. When she put her arm
on his shoulder, he shrunk back, but didn't move away.

"Lee, I see Vic gave you four new cars. One is a gold Jaguar. One is a
sleek, blue racing car. Another is a green Jeep. And the fourth is quite the
winner—a black, shiny limousine. Do you know why Vic gave you those
presents? It's not your birthday. Any idea?"

"He likes cars. He saved them in his room."

"Yes, he likes what you like. But something even more important,
Lee. He loves you," Deirdre said emphatically. "Do you know what that
means?"

"He loves me," Lee repeated. "Vic loves me. Vic loves me."

It was hard to know what the word *love* meant to Lee. Was it like he

was acting in a play, repeating his mother's words as if he was following her script? Was he aware that his brother had feelings about him?
For starters, he did seem to know his brother had a point of view. He
assumed it was the same as his: Vic likes cars. Surely, this was a spectac-
ular gain for him to know that Vic liked things that he saved. Knowledge
of emotions, however, was of a vastly different order. That still needed
extensive work. Lee was only four, and if he was going to grasp even just
a few emotions, it would take time. He acted angry, scared, anxious, and
happy. Deirdre wanted him to know the words for those emotions. His
singing was his most emotional behavior. He sang with Wade during
the getting-dressed game, but he also sang by himself, blocking everyone
out, like the night she yelled at him.

Remembering the singing incident, Deirdre had one more idea.
She wanted Lee to ultimately learn how to be part of the family, which
meant adjusting to what other members of the family needed. This was
a long-term goal that would take years, but as a start, they could address
turn-taking. His preschool took issue that he was not sharing, yet to
Deirdre, this seemed like a far-reaching expectation. But taking turns at
home could be a start.

One Saturday night, Deirdre gathered everyone to watch the music
video Lee enjoyed. Everyone was game to make this a successful night.
There was popcorn and pizza—a regular party. She had printed out the
lyrics to the song that only Lee had memorized. After the show, she told
Lee there was a new rule for singing the song: each person would sing
one line when she pointed to them and then the next person would sing
the next line. Lee did not understand this instruction at first. He had
to see it in action. But he was interested in singing, so he waited and
watched as Deirdre handed everyone a paper with the song printed out.
She had put names next to each line. It was a short song, about eight
lines that repeated. Lee couldn't read, but when Deirdre pointed to each
person when it was their turn to sing, Lee learned the rule. As usual, Lee
liked rules and followed them exactly.

Dad and Vic had terrible voices, but they didn't care; they thought their singing was truly funny. The plan worked. Lee only sang his line when Deirdre pointed at him. He never lost interest, but after about four stanzas, everyone else did. Nevertheless, Lee had learned turn-taking. At least, this time.

Deirdre and Carl knew that Lee couldn't generalize everything he learned and transfer it to new situations. Turn-taking, learning an emotional vocabulary, playing with his brothers, and caring how he looked would have to come up repeatedly. Without careful instruction, he wouldn't know that rules varied depending on the context. But eventually, what he learned would stick. It was rote knowledge sometimes, and he would do things at first because they were scripted, but it enabled him to enter the social world and live a less restricted life.

Lee was a part of something more than himself; he was a member of his family. Carl and Deirdre sensed he knew that.

Chapter Seven

Jealousy in an Identical Twin

Six-Year-Old Clive

Laughing heartily for minutes without stopping, six-year-old Clive and his mother cuddled outdoors on a weather-beaten lounge watching a comical scene from *Finding Nemo* on their iPad. This was Clive's favorite animated movie, and he'd watched it many times. The way mother and son looked at each other as they laughed revealed their warm tie. Clive's mother looked into his squinting brown eyes, caught his gaze, and reveled in it. Her eyebrows rose and her eyes widened, reflecting her pleasure in his glee. They were in sync with each other's movements, a telltale sign of their close bond.

Because Clive had seemed a little downtrodden of late, his mother was enjoying this upbeat moment with him. Nearby, Ari—Clive's always-cheery identical twin—was shooting hoops with his father, aiming at a basketball net at kid's height, shouting happily each time he scored. Ari was the more flamboyant twin, especially when emboldened by his father's exuberant presence and admiration. This was a rather typical set of interactions for the Richards family. Since the boys were babies, Mrs. Richards, who was slight of build but sturdy in personal confidence, nurtured Clive, who needed gentle attention. He fussed a lot, had a harder time sleeping through the night, and needed to be nursed more often as an infant. Mr. Richards, tall and athletic, had deferred to his wife when it came to parenting newborns, but pitched in with Ari, who was a bubbly, active, easygoing infant. It all seemed natural because Mrs. Richards was a quiet, sensitive parent while Mr. Richards was more rambunctious. It was a sunny day for everyone because their family time was not being interrupted by the frequent, long business trips Mr. Richards had been taking recently.

Although the twins looked nearly identical, they were definitely not alike. Undoubtedly, they had a close, caring connection, but their interests and personalities were different. They were in the same kindergarten class and would turn six midyear. It was springtime—just two-and-a-half months left to the term. At the beginning of the year, Clive had been less able to adjust to school than his more outgoing and flexible twin. Clive was still behind Ari, who had already learned to read. However, he had responded positively to his warmhearted teacher, who had coaxed him along socially and academically as the year sped ahead. Clive liked her very much and felt protected by her presence.

However, this experienced, perceptive teacher was concerned by a change she had lately noticed in Clive. Something had come over him. He had begun hitting Ari during class. Early in the year, the boys had chosen to sit next to each other. Her inclination would have been to set them apart, but she knew they gravitated to each other, and so she let the seating arrangement slide. Now it seemed to be a problem. If Ari raised his hand and was chosen before Clive, Clive would give him a little swipe on his shoulder. Then the struggle seemed to spread to the playground. If Ari was chosen for a playground game before his brother, Clive seemed upset and would give his brother a quick, but forceful, tap on the back. While surprised, Ari was never retaliatory. He just walked away. The teacher asked Clive what was wrong, but he just said, "I don't know." She told him to apologize, which he did automatically and perfunctorily. He was a polite and good-natured child, so these reactions seemed strange for him.

Meanwhile, the situation at home mirrored that at school. Clive lashed out in reaction to the attention his father gave to Ari. Mr. Richards had been on a month-long trip, and Mrs. Richards and the twins coped with his absence with daily phone calls and emails. Clive began hitting Ari when Mr. Richards returned. Like his teacher, his mother was protective of Clive.

When the hitting began at home, it also increased in school, and the teacher called the Richards in for a conference. She admitted that perhaps she had been too protective of Clive and felt that a consequence for his behavior was needed. Clive's father agreed, but his mother was more tentative. The next day, when Clive hit his brother, the teacher sat Clive down and explained that his hitting had to stop. As a result of his action, she explained, he would lose the privilege of painting that day. Painting was his favorite activity, the one area in which he stood out. A precocious artist, he had the ability to draw using perspective, which was unusual for his age.

Although the teacher acted immediately and fully explained her actions, Clive's hitting didn't stop. Her idea that punishment might teach him a lesson didn't work. Both she and Clive's parents were confounded, so she referred the Richards to the school psychologist, who alerted the parents to Parental Intelligence. The psychologist reviewed the process and the Richards enrolled in a course at their local library.

STEP ONE
Stepping Back

When Mrs. Richards tried to step back, her feelings rushed in, and she couldn't bear them at first. Instead of thinking about Clive, her frustration about her husband's frequent, long absences surged forward. These thoughts so preoccupied her that she was blind to what was happening to her son.

Mr. and Mrs. Richards had tried to talk about the business trips before, but now she knew they had to discuss them further. Mr. Richards held firmly to his explanation that there had to be at least three more lengthy trips that year to land an important new contract for his company which they needed to avoid a major downturn in profits. Without the new contract, Mr. Richards feared they might have to take out a second mortgage they couldn't afford. Mrs. Richards understood the practicality of his plan, but it didn't relieve her aggravation. Taking care of both boys day and night during his absences had been a lonely struggle. She worked in a department store while the boys were at school and came home tired only to deal with this new problem. It seemed too much.

Mr. Richards reminded her that the point of stepping back was for them to review Clive's situation together. Since his trips weren't going to change for some time, they had to take the opportunity they had while he was home to track the hitting episodes. Mrs. Richards finally understood that stepping back would help her focus on Clive's actions.

She recalled that before her husband left for his last trip, Clive held back as Ari hugged and kissed his father good-bye. She asked, "I wonder what Clive was feeling? Why was he so standoffish?"

Mr. Richards said, "I remember saying good-bye to Ari, too. He ran up to me at the door, hugged me tightly, and said how much he would miss me. Clive was more sullen, reserved. He stood back, like you said. I did say good-bye to him when he didn't approach me, and gave him a kiss on the cheek, but he didn't really respond. He stood so still."

"I remember that," Mrs. Richards said. "Clive seemed gloomy. I put my arms around him as you pulled out of the driveway."

They realized this pattern repeated itself every time Mr. Richards called home. Ari would rush to the phone while Clive held back, waiting for his mother to offer him the phone. Sometimes he just went to his room without a word to his father. When Mr. Richards came home, he would hug Ari while Clive turned away and went into the kitchen. Mr. Richards gave him his space and did not speak to him. Mr. Richards said he felt rebuffed.

Only by stepping back did both parents see clearly that Clive was repeatedly distancing himself from his father. They also discussed how it was possible that Clive didn't understand the reason for the teacher's punishment. He didn't connect losing the privilege of painting to his hitting. Too much was on his mind. They decided to review several of the hitting episodes in slow motion to see if they would find other repetitive patterns. They focused on the situations at home. They recalled that one day, when Clive hit Ari, Mr. Richards had just been bike riding with Ari. On another day, Clive hit Ari when his father and Ari were watching television together.

Mr. and Mrs. Richards refrained from making a judgment about Clive's misbehavior before they completed the process of trying to understand it. This parenting mindset helped them reconsider how Clive was the more passive twin. Even in utero, they noticed on an ultrasound that Ari was the more active baby. In other words, their differences in temperament began prenatally. With this in mind, Mrs. Richards was naturally beginning to reflect on Clive's earliest experiences.

STEP TWO
Self-Reflecting

Mrs. Richards began to revisit her early maternal experience. She and her husband didn't know they were having twins until the ultrasound in week twenty. Their date of delivery was uncertain because one of the twins, Clive, wasn't developing well in utero. He was smaller than Ari, and her obstetrician warned her to be prepared for a possible early induction if he didn't seem to be growing well. As it happened, however, an early delivery was not necessary.

Each twin had a dramatically different first week of life. Clive, at five pounds, was placed in the Intensive Care Unit and fed by a nasogastric tube due to difficulties with sucking. Mrs. Richards was told his mouth was "too flat to suckle" and his growth needed careful monitoring. In his first week, Clive mostly slept. Ari—six pounds, four ounces—remained with his mother and was breastfed. Mrs. Richards spent as much time as she could by Clive's side giving him some physical care. While it was easier to become connected to Ari's lusty responsiveness, she was also getting connected to Clive through her intense worry and longing for him. She felt left out of the quiet world he was dwelling in.

It was all too easy for Mrs. Richards to project her own lonesome world as a child to her silent, sleeping infant. She was born to immigrant parents who only spoke English to her because they wanted her to be Americanized, but in the evenings, they often spoke their native language to each other. She was left out because she couldn't understand what they were saying. As an only child, she often felt alone in her small family when her parents went into their own linguistic world. Her sleeping infant returned her to a time when she felt the longing to communicate with someone who was present but vocally absent.

Once both twins were home and breastfeeding, they each seemed to form a separate bond with their mother. Mrs. Richards continued to worry about Clive, even though he was quite healthy. By about seven months, the twins seemed actively aware of each other, and by twenty months, they were playmates. Mrs. Richards was so actively involved with them that they didn't develop the interdependence often typical of twins who favor each other over their mother. However, as if to avoid rivalry and subsequent hostility, they seemed to accept a kind of complementarity in that Clive was submissive to Ari's demonstrative leadership.

Mr. Richards silently felt that his wife was overprotective of Clive. He felt a kinship with Ari's personality and could relate to him more easily than to his other son. He observed that his wife spent more time in Clive's room before sleep than with his brother. She sat with him when he did his homework because he had difficulties with it, and they took walks together. While Mr. Richards felt his wife favored Clive, he openly recognized that he favored Ari. He liked his spunk and openness. On the other hand, he found Clive a conundrum and backed off from trying to get close to him as he got older, a pattern that started when his wife gave Clive special care as an infant. Roughhousing with Ari was more his speed.

This roughhousing reminded Mr. Richards of growing up in a house with six brothers. They were always tumbling about. They weren't particularly close to their parents. In fact, he realized he didn't know his parents well at all. The brothers formed a tight social bond that was fostered by his parents. None of the sons was prized for his individuality. Both parents worked long hours, barely making ends meet, and the brothers took care of each other. The older boys had dinner ready when their parents got home, and all the brothers did their homework together, watched TV, and went to bed. They followed their parents' rules, did their chores, and seemed to solve their own arguments remarkably well. His parents were quiet people; feelings weren't discussed in the family.

Mr. Richards was surprised his sons didn't roughhouse together or have similar personalities, especially since they were twins. But he thought that his wife's early worries about differences in their beginnings set the tone. When she was with Clive as a baby, he'd often pick up Ari. One day, he realized that Clive's distance hurt and that he didn't know how to make a loving connection with him. He shared these thoughts with his wife and, during their discussion, realized with shame that he resented Clive for not being more like himself.

Mrs. Richards appreciated her husband's openness. She realized in retrospect that she had been feeling disappointed by her husband's distance from Clive and accepted her role in fostering their respective roles with each twin. Clive and her husband were both missing out. She conceded that to help her husband tackle his relationship with Clive meant she had to give them emotional room to discover each other. Her husband was affected by his wife's heartfelt wish for him to strengthen his tie to Clive and realized that his parents' distance when he was a child was not a good fit for his own family. He had to think about how to go the extra mile with Clive.

STEP THREE
Understanding Your Child's Mind

During the month he was working from home before his next trip, Mr. Richards decided to observe Clive more closely. Kindergarten homework took longer than Mr. Richards had ever imagined, and it entailed parent participation, something he hadn't been involved in thus far. An example was timing each boy as he read a long list of sight words. He watched as his wife timed Ari, and he completed the list quickly because he knew every word. She then told Ari to go in the other room to complete the rest of the work on his own. When she called Clive into the kitchen, he procrastinated, claiming he was busy with his Legos. She waited ten minutes, then gave him a five-minute warning. She purposefully did not have the boys do their work together because she didn't want Clive to watch Ari's performance, which was better than Clive's would be. When Mrs. Richards called a second time, Clive came in promptly. He struggled with about half the words, so Mrs. Richards stopped timing; it only made him anxious. He eventually read the list in the required time and went back in the other room to join his brother and complete the other assignment. In a notebook, the boys were required to draw a line from a word to a picture. Then, they had to draw a picture of whatever they chose and dictate a story about the picture, which a parent would write for them on a separate sheet of paper.

When Clive was working on the second assignment, Mr. Richards noticed him get up several times to look over Ari's shoulder. He realized Clive wasn't trying to copy his brother's work; instead, he wanted to see how far Ari had gotten. Although Ari was way ahead because he'd started fifteen minutes earlier, it was evident to Clive that his brother had no difficulty completing the exercise. Clive left the room with his head down. His notebook was left open on the dining room table, his work unfinished.

Mr. Richards waited a few minutes, then looked around to find Clive. He saw him working intently at the computer in a small office that everyone used. He stood back, curious about what Clive was doing. He could see from a distance that he had located a painting program and was busy engineering a picture. Mr. Richards didn't know that Clive was capable of using the computer, let alone navigating a painting application. He realized how much he didn't know about his son's abilities. He didn't want to disturb him, so he left the room and came back twenty minutes later to find Clive still busy with his design. He asked Clive if he could look at his painting, but Clive quickly shut down the computer.

"Clive," Mr. Richards said, "I didn't know you were such a computer guy. You're quite the tech wizard. Can I ask what program you were using?"

"Oh, it's just Microsoft Paint," Clive replied and turned his head to the side, away from his father.

"How'd you learn to use it?" Mr. Richards asked with excitement.

"I don't know. I just did it. It shows you paintbrushes and colors, and you just choose and draw," said Clive softly.

"That's amazing, Clive! Could I take a little peek at your painting?"

"I don't know. You might get mad at me," answered Clive timidly.

Mr. Richards was surprised. He'd never had a real conversation with either boy about their feelings. Clive was so direct about this that Mr. Richards was taken aback. He'd never gotten mad at either boy. He didn't even raise his voice, except when he was having a good time. *But that's usually with Ari,* Mr. Richards thought with regret. It wasn't like he never played with Clive, but he just didn't enjoy Legos as much and found it hard to play with him. He recalled they did like biking together. Why didn't he do more of that?

Mr. Richards responded the only way he knew how. "Clive, I'm never mad at you. I can't think of anything you could do to get me mad. A painting won't make me mad. I promise."

Clive looked straight at his father. He paused for quite a while, as if what his father said might not be true. He was still worried, but he knew that his father never yelled at him, so he hesitantly opened the computer and, with a click, his drawing popped up:

Mr. Richards was shocked when he looked and saw his name on Clive's picture. He didn't know anything about children's drawings, but clearly this was about him and Clive.

"Clive, I see your name and my name. Yours is so big. Mine is so small. What am I doing? Can you tell me?" Mr. Richards asked.

"You are going away for a long time," whispered Clive.

"Okay," Mr. Richards said, worried. "Where am I going?"

"I don't know," Clive replied, his brow wrinkled.

"Well, if you don't know, does anyone know?" Mr. Richards wondered out loud, trying to be as sensitive as he knew how. Actually, Mr. Richards was a very sensitive guy, not only to others but also about himself. He had his own feelings hurt quite easily, and that was why he had felt rebuffed by Clive when he came home from his trip. He assumed Clive wasn't particularly interested in him; his son's picture showed him that he was wrong.

His name was written in small letters, while the daddy figure was big. Something about that struck him as important. He'd have to think more about that later because although Clive had paused to consider his father's question, he was answering it now:

"I think Mommy knows," Clive answered, slumping in his seat. "She knows why, and she won't tell me."

"Why won't she tell you?" Mr. Richards asked quietly, totally confounded, and even scared. He thought that his little son was shouldering something of momentous importance, and here they were alone, without his wife, who would definitely be more understanding about all this.

"Because I'm bad, and she doesn't want to hurt my feelings," Clive replied. "She's nice even when I'm bad. But my teacher isn't anymore."

"Oh. What did your teacher do?" Mr. Richards felt that the conversation was going well, but he didn't know where it was leading. All he knew was that he felt incredibly sad for his little boy. He was only six and had such big, upsetting ideas.

"She told me I couldn't paint. I like to paint. I like to paint very much. Daddy, I want to paint in school." Clive started to cry and climbed onto his father's lap.

Clive had never climbed into his lap before. This was a mommy thing. Mr. Richards sensed his son was beside himself with grief. He suddenly felt so close to Clive, and even though he knew his son was so distressed, he knew something positive was happening between them. From the classes on Parental Intelligence, he knew that understanding his son's mind was paramount.

Mr. Richards looked back at the picture for more clues. He was very tempted to call his wife but sensed he shouldn't. This was between Clive and himself. He plunged in. "Clive, why did the teacher say you couldn't paint?"

"It's because I'm bad like I told you." Clive paused and then blurted out, "I hit Ari. More than once, too. That is bad. Really bad. And you went away. Far away."

"Clive, do you think I went away because you hit Ari?" Mr. Richards asked in fear.

"No. You went away because I can't read. You don't like boys who can't read. You like smart boys like Ari."

Mr. Richards found himself rocking Clive very slowly like a baby. He was speechless, having trouble following his son's gloomy logic. He didn't know what he had done to cause Clive to think he didn't like him. But then he thought again. It wasn't what he had done. It was what he hadn't done. He had never paid enough attention to Clive, so Clive drew the conclusion that he didn't like him. Then, he speculated, when Clive had a problem reading—which wasn't really a problem, except in comparison to Ari—Clive imagined that his father didn't like him because of the reading, and had therefore gone away. It was an outlandish conclusion, but it followed the logic of a child's mind.

Then, before he could speak, Clive added another part of the puzzle. "Daddy, it's okay. Don't be upset. I don't like me either because I can't read."

Mr. Richards was tearing up. His son, his remarkably sensitive son, was consoling him! He had to speak now and be very clear.

"Clive," he said slowly. "I went away to make money for all of us. I never go away because I don't like you. I like you very much. I love you very much."

Clive stared at his father, who continued, "Lots of kids don't read when they are in kindergarten. You can take as long as you need to learn. It's not a race to see who can read first."

"But the teacher said I couldn't paint because I can't read."

"Clive, she didn't say that," Mr. Richards explained. "She didn't know why you were hitting and thought if you didn't get to paint, you would stop hitting."

"What does painting have to do with hitting?" Clive asked, befuddled. "I don't hit when I paint. That's impossible!"

Mr. Richards couldn't restrain himself. He laughed, and Clive smiled, relieved his father found something, anything, funny about all this. Clive's body relaxed, and he looked at his father with curiosity.

"Clive," Mr. Richards asked, "did you hit Ari because the teacher would call on him to read?"

"My teacher was always my friend, but then she started calling on Ari a lot. More than on me. I thought she liked him more because he could read so well. That made me mad, so I hit Ari."

"Gotcha," his father said. Pointing at the picture, he asked. "Clive, what are you doing here?"

"Will you write the story if I tell it to you?"

"Absolutely. Let's do it," Mr. Richards responded, immediately standing up to get some paper and a pen. "Go for it, pal."

Clive began telling his story. "There was a boy falling off his chair because he couldn't read the words in his notebook. His brother knew more words than he did. He felt like crying, and he did. Little tears."

Mr. Richards instantly saw the little tears coming from his son's eyes in the picture that he had missed before.

Clive continued. "He thought his father was mad at him. He thought he was leaving because he was mad that his twin son didn't know his words. But he thought wrong. His daddy was going to work. The end."

Mr. Richards wrote as fast as he could to keep up with Clive's rapid dictation. He smiled. Clive knew that he wasn't mad and he was going to work. Terrific! Clive had understood their talk. He was incredibly pleased. But he heard the word *twin*, which was unexpected, and he became very curious.

"Clive," Mr. Richards asked, "what does being a 'twin' mean?"

Clive's forehead became furrowed as he stared into space.

"I think other people think it means two brothers are the same when they're not. Brothers can look alike to people even when they look different to each other. But, anyway, looking alike and being alike aren't the same thing. I think, because Ari is my twin, my teacher expects me to read like he does. I don't. Kids think Ari can draw and paint because I do. He can't. Daddy, did you know all that?"

"Yes, Clive, I know all that," Mr. Richards replied. "But I don't expect you and Ari to be the same. You can like some of the same things and not like other things. You can each find some things easier to do than other things. You are brothers in the same family with the same mommy and daddy and—"

"Daddy," Clive interrupted, "I know we are in the same family with you and Mommy. Duh!"

Mr. Richards laughed. "Sorry. Of course, you know that. So being twins means you are the same age, but everything else isn't the same all the time."

"Right," Clive said. "I'm hungry. Can I finish my homework after we eat dinner?" Clive was ending their discussion. He found out what he needed to know. Relieved, he could attend to being hungry.

"Sure," Mr. Richards said, grinning. "Would you like me to sit with you when you finish your notebook after dinner?"

"Will you? Okay," Clive crowed. "And then I have to draw another picture, too. Can we write another story?"

"You got it."

Clive gave his father a big hug; he had never left his lap.

Later in the evening, after the boys had gone to sleep, Mr. Richards told his wife about his talk with Clive, what he had learned about Clive's incorrect conclusions, and how his assumptions were changed by their discussion. He told her that, in Clive's picture, his name was written in small letters. He said he had wondered what it meant. With careful thought, he shared with her that he speculated that Clive drew the letters of his name so tiny because he hadn't been around that much lately. It touched him deeply. He believed that writing his name that way was a result of his frequent absences combined with his emotional distance from Clive when he was at home. She was deeply moved and complimented him on being such a perceptive father. She added that she now understood Clive's reluctance to talk to him on the phone or when he returned from the trip. From Clive's perspective, his father was too mad at him to want to talk with him.

Both parents were certain that understanding their son's mind would guide them with his future struggles. They became much more alert to Clive's jealousy of Ari. It appeared to be his precocious reading ability that led to his false conclusion that his father liked Ari more, but maybe there was more to it than that. They had a lot to think about. Because the twins got along so well generally, they had missed the importance of hidden jealousies that they would now be more sensitive to.

STEP FOUR
Understanding Your Child's Development

The Richards reviewed Clive's development. He had just turned six when the hitting episodes began. Previously, the teacher had told them he had succeeded in the major tasks of kindergarten: he was well behaved, he was capable of socialization, and he enjoyed learning. They realized he was generally able to maintain self-control and flexibility, except under great stress, as evidenced by his hitting. They now recognized that his relationships had a bearing on his self-control and resiliency, specifically due to his insecure attachment to his father.

They were pleased that Clive had a sense of right and wrong, knew how to follow rules, and had even shown precocious mastery in his complex achievement: painting. He got along with the children in his class, knew how to play and share with others, and sought approval from his teacher, with whom he had a positive relationship. The teacher said he was learning to write well, his language and motor skills were on track, and he was developing reading readiness. She was pleased that he was meeting all the developmental expectations of his age.

The Richards were proud of his achievements. They knew now that what had gone amiss was his relationship with his father. Mr. Richards recognized that he had underestimated his role at this age. He took it upon himself to read about father-son relationships at six years old. He discovered that boys at that age watch their fathers closely so they can identify with their behaviors and attitudes and seek their love and approval. Mr. Richards realized that even though he had not previously favored Clive nor sought him out, Clive was still attached to him. Mrs. Richards agreed, adding that she had read that attachment is not always derived from satisfying relations. She told her husband that she had discovered in her reading that attachment can be motivated by stress as well as pleasure. Thus, Clive's desire to be close to him, although not based on a positive tie like the one with Ari, was still there all along.

Together, Clive's parents figured out that the emotional distance between Mr. Richards and Clive had stirred up Clive's strong need for him, and because of their lack of a solid relationship, this need spiraled out of control and nobody else could substitute. Mrs. Richards recognized that her love and adoration could not replace the love and adoration from her husband. Clive's goal was to be close to his father emotionally and physically. They both regretted that Clive's anger and sadness had come with the lack of these experiences. Clive's unexpected behavior—hitting—eventually brought him closer to his father because his father had discussed it with him so warmly over Clive's drawing.

STEP FIVE
Problem Solving

The Richards realized that the hitting problem was solved, but many underlying problems had surfaced that they needed to attend to continuously. They thought the boys competed with each other about their achievements, especially Clive, whose focus on reading revealed that he was closely watching Ari's easier and faster progress at school. Ari didn't envy the abilities Clive had that he didn't, such as Clive's artistic talents. However, they wondered how Ari might feel if they encouraged Clive to be more demonstrative about his interests instead of taking the backseat to Ari's leadership qualities. Both boys could play basketball, ride bikes, and swim well. There was no reason to assume Ari would be better at these sports. Mr. Richards just hadn't encouraged Clive thus far and thought he should. In fact, Mr. Richards asked his wife to hold back what looked like her overprotective behavior with Clive. He wasn't a baby anymore, and he would probably blossom if she didn't treat him like he needed her so much. She conceded that her husband was right. She was projecting her needs as a child for more affection and involvement from her parents onto Clive.

Mr. Richards began to play sports with both boys as if they were a little team. In their athletic abilities, the twins were pretty much on a par with each other. The boys began shooting hoops and riding bikes together more often while Mr. Richards was at work. They seemed to enjoy each other and boosted each other's skills with this practice; they weren't as competitive as their parents imagined. Ari had no problem letting Clive take the lead at times. They took turns, readily deciding who should go first when they played different games. At school, the teacher noticed that Clive was participating more in class and on the playground, and there was less pressure for Ari to always be number one.

Mr. and Mrs. Richards made sure that each parent had alone time with each boy, and both got to know both their sons better. One major problem still remained—Mr. Richards's upcoming trips. They thought this should be a family discussion. One night, at dinner, Mr. Richards took the initiative:

"Clive and Ari, next week I will be going away again for a three-week work trip. I will be flying on a plane next Saturday morning, and I wondered if we could all go to the airport together so you can see me off."

Clive reacted quickly, "Daddy, I don't want you to go. Do you have to?"

"Unfortunately, in my work, I have to meet with people in person to sell them on my ideas. I'm planning to build a new shopping mall, and I have to give what's called a PowerPoint presentation. That means I show them pictures on a large computer screen about the building plans and have several screen pages, called slides, of the major reasons why this mall should be built. I can't just talk to them on the phone. Showing them pictures and giving them my reasons in person influences their decisions."

"Wow, Daddy. It's like you're an artist. Can we see the pictures, too?" Clive asked with enthusiasm.

"Ari, would you like that, too?" Mr. Richards asked, including his other son in the discussion.

"Sure, Daddy," replied Ari, smiling.

"I'd like to see the show, too!" Mrs. Richards exclaimed. "I've seen some of the plans, but not the actual presentation. But before we do that,

I think we should talk about how we all feel when we are apart and what we can do when we all miss Daddy and he misses us."

Clive took the lead again. "I think we should FaceTime on our—"

"—iPads, so we can see each other," Ari chimed in.

"That's what I was gonna say!" Clive said.

Once again, Mr. Richards was surprised by Clive's computer knowledge. Apparently, Ari knew about FaceTime, too, because in school they met another class in another country by using FaceTime.

"What a great idea," Mrs. Richards said. "You two are the best long-distance planners. This is going to be great. Let's do it every night when Daddy is away, unless he's at a dinner meeting and gets in past bedtime. Okay, everyone?"

"Yeah," Clive and Ari said at once. Then Ari said, looking at Clive, "Mommy, we want to bring the dishes into the kitchen later and—"

"—watch Daddy's pictures now," Clive finished.

She agreed readily, and the family gathered around the computer to see the slides Mr. Richards had prepared. He showed them all the pictures and read some of the simpler sales pitches.

On the day they were leaving for the airport, everyone was a bit solemn. Three weeks was a long time. Before Mr. Richards went through security, Clive rushed up to him, hugged him vigorously, and said, "I'm going to miss you, Daddy."

"I'll miss you, too, Clive, and we'll FaceTime tonight for the first time." Then he hugged Ari, telling him the same thing. Before leaving with his suitcases, he gave his wife a hug, too, and then headed into the security line.

Mrs. Richards looked closely at her boys as they watched their father disappear. Upon leaving the airport, the boys started chasing each other happily. As she ran after them, she thought how lucky her boys were to have her husband as their father. Not that life would always go smoothly, but their openness with each other felt extraordinary.

Chapter Eight

The Storm, the Calm with ADHD

Eight-Year-Old Cathie

It was a brisk fall in a small southwestern Nebraska town midway between Denver and Omaha on the Republican River. The town had a friendly, front-porch culture. Lia and Dale Wicar and their eight-year-old daughter, Cathie, lived in a sturdy wooden house shaded by maple and ash trees and surrounded by prairie. Dale and Lia made their living by supplying farmers with implements and equipment, including tractors and harvesters. Lia did the bookkeeping while Cathie was in school, and Dale ran their dealership, including the thriving repair shop.

The Wicars made a good parenting team, sharing with Cathie their love of country-western music and reading good books. Their church was the center of their social lives, and they enjoyed going to the high school's sporting events with friends and neighbors. Lia was a devout Christian who taught at the Sunday School Cathie attended. Dale was an agnostic, but they shared common values about kindness to others and a generous spirit. Dale didn't put much stock in the Bible, but he kept this to himself, so Lia could take the lead in their daughter's religious upbringing. He was a well-meaning, modest, common-sense kind of fellow.

Lia believed in being a kind but firm mother. When she said no, she expected her daughter to listen promptly. She learned this from her French mother and felt it helped her grow up "properly." At the same time, she believed in letting Cathie make many of her own choices—like picking out her clothes, choosing her friends, and deciding on her interests—so she could feel independent and figure things out on her own. Lia knew that she gained a lifetime's supply of self-confidence when her own mother did this for her. But when it came to certain things, like manners or respect for others or education, Lia strictly ruled in a calm but forthright manner. She believed homework should be checked and rechecked and handed in on time and letter-perfect. This led to always doing your best and having pride in your work.

Dale often argued with Lia about her parenting approach. To him, what Lia called *firm* actually felt cold, and he believed that Cathie needed warm encouragement instead. While he, too, felt education was important, he had a more relaxed attitude. He felt that inspiration grew from the pleasure of learning.

Cathie and her father were very close. They spent a lot of time together playing, and Lia often reined them in to make sure that her rules were followed. Consequently, Cathie and her mother were in battle mode frequently. Cathie had a great deal of energy and always seemed to be in motion. Sitting still did not fit her personality. Cathie was disorganized; Lia was neat as a pin. Cathie and her mother also disagreed about the frequent snacks Cathie asked for. They bickered about Cathie's unruly hair, which, like the rest of her, was never in one place for very long. And they squabbled because Cathie was rushing, when instead, she should be carefully getting ready each morning to get to the school bus on time. Mother and daughter were like oil and water—an impossible combination.

Mother and daughter argued at meal times about how long Cathie had to sit at the table. In fact, a typical dinner was filled with Cathie not following Lia's rules. Good homemade food would be passed around the table. Cathie would take small portions and eat quickly for less than ten minutes. Then she'd get out of her seat and stand, chatting merrily. Lia would ask her to sit down, and Cathie would comply—for all of five minutes. This cycle would repeat until Lia would become indignant and scold Cathie, who, by this time, would be bouncing on her seat. Trying to support his wife, Dale would urge Cathie to finish her meal, but Cathie would announce she had eaten enough, look imploringly at her mother, and skip out of the kitchen. Lia and Dale would finish their dinner quietly, recovering from the usual tempest—their daughter.

Toward the end of second grade, Cathie was diagnosed with attention-deficit/hyperactivity disorder, or ADHD. This diagnosis gave the Wicars a new frame of reference for their daughter's disorganization, constant motion, and trouble focusing and concentrating for solid lengths of time. Lia wasn't too proud to realize that her style didn't suit her daughter and that she needed to learn to adapt to her daughter's disorder. She looked to her faith to give her the strength to find new ways to help her daughter. She also believed that she could find and follow new parenting paths. She began by telling Dale that she would consider their parenting differences, that they both had a lot to learn, and that they needed to do this together. They knew they could rely on their strong marital bond to find a way to parent Cathie effectively.

Cathie was in a muddle about being classified as someone with a problem. Even though her doctor and parents had explained why she had to take medicine, she had not been able to fully understand what it was that made her dissimilar from her peers. By third grade, she just knew she felt different. She was embarrassed when she had to leave the classroom for reading help. She wished she were smarter.

Cathie's medication was a stimulant designed to help her concentrate, but despite the medicine, she was still disorganized. By the time her classmates had hung up their coats, gotten their books from their cubbies, and begun the board work, Cathie was still ruffling through papers she forgot to bring home or looking for a misplaced book. A typical day started with her teacher helping her settle down by organizing her things, but that meant that Cathie arrived at her desk already feeling like an outsider.

Cathie's medication wore off by the time she got home. Because this stimulant took away her appetite, her lunch box was still filled with food, and she was "starving." Lia understood that the medication had this effect on her daughter. She therefore never mentioned the full lunch box and always had a sandwich ready when Cathie got home. Perplexed about how to get her daughter to begin her homework, she allowed her to go outside to play for an hour to have some fun and work off some energy.

Each day seemed to run on a similar course. Cathie was in a good mood and having fun when she was called in. She generally only had about twenty minutes of homework if she could concentrate, but as Lia now expected, Cathie couldn't sit still for more than a few minutes. Lia tried to keep her focused. She didn't care if Cathie worked standing up or sitting down, which was a big shift for Lia, but nonetheless, every day both mother and daughter ended up very tense.

One day, one of Cathie's assignments was to write a few sentences about a story they had read in school. After writing only one, she ran around the room. Lia used her old firm style and determinedly told Cathie to come back to the table. Cathie understood her mother's tone and returned. She wrote one more sentence and then her complaints began and quickly rose to a high pitch.

"I'm still hungry."

"After your work is done, we'll have dinner."

"I hate reading."

"I know it's hard. Just two more sentences and four math problems."

Cathie ran over to her toys. "I just have to play a little bit."

Lia lost her cool. "Get back here!"

"I can't, I can't," Cathie cried out, landing with her tummy flat out on the floor with her arms over her head. She began to sob.

"Crying won't work. Ten more minutes," Lia said, picking Cathie up and putting her on her chair.

Cathie grumbled sadly, "I'm so stupid." She got up from her chair more slowly this time, crawled under the table, and curled up into a ball.

Lia was worn out and depleted. "That's it. No dessert tonight and bed at seven. You'll get up early tomorrow morning to finish."

Cathie and her mother couldn't control Cathie's ADHD, and that afternoon, they felt lost and hopeless with each other. Cathie went to play, and Lia realized that completing the homework would indeed have to wait for the morning. Lia went on her computer to find a mother blog that might relieve her. She didn't actually want to be punitive. Taking something away from Cathie was an impulsive, irritated reaction. Going to bed early and finishing in the morning might have been a wise choice since Cathie was given new medicine at 7:00 a.m., but reacting too quickly and out of frustration was a problem. Whatever happened to her calm demeanor?

Reading blogs often helped Lia regain her composure. She found she wasn't alone in trying to figure out how to parent. In one of the posts by a parent who also had a child with ADHD, she found a link to another post, "Parental Intelligence." A few clicks later, she found an archive of articles detailing the five steps to Parental Intelligence. She was struck by the firmness and confidence in the examples of parents who used this approach. This appealed to her. It seemed to make sense to her to follow the five steps. Reading about it gave her back her innate sense of order. She was ready to share with Dale the first idea: stepping back.

━━━━━━━━━━

STEP ONE
Stepping Back

Eight-year-old Cathie didn't mean to be provocative, but her running around and climbing under the table caused a lot of tension and anger in Lia. The homework situation recurred every day after school. The cumulative effect of so many days of battle had worn Lia down. It felt good to recognize this because she was feeling so ineffective.

The next day, Lia began to consider what was reasonable to accomplish when the medicine was wearing off. She realized she had time to do what the blog recommended: step back to think about her reactions and feelings. There was no immediate emergency or crisis, though Cathie's restlessness made it feel like one. That was her first revelation. Then she realized she was taking Cathie's actions personally and felt disrespected—her second revelation. It wasn't really personal. She knew Cathie was both respectful and good-natured, and she was certainly not out to get her mother upset. But Lia was tired from the effort it took to help her daughter with basic tasks like homework.

She decided to reconstruct the previous afternoon and make sense of it. Rewinding her mental clock to the time Cathie came home from school the day before, she began to recreate the events that led to their mutual frustration. She quickly realized that she was developing a different frame of mind. Lia recalled how happy Cathie was when she came home from school—how delighted she was to eat her sandwich and run outside to play. She readily came in to do her homework, but then rapidly lost her focus. Lia realized how quickly Cathie could go from being cheerful and calm to anxious and disorganized. Stepping back helped her see this transformation.

Lia had hoped the punishment of taking away Cathie's dessert, her favorite part of the meal, would teach Cathie that she must calm down so homework was done, but in retrospect, it was evident that Cathie already knew this; she just had trouble following through. Reviewing the sequence of events, Lia was able to come to different conclusions. She remembered Cathie asking if she could play for a few minutes for a break from the homework. Lia decided that, the next time that happened, she would get on the floor with Cathie to take a little break and have fun, in her husband's style. Lia's gentle, sensitive side was coming forth.

Suspending her judgment, she realized Cathie's getting under the table the day before wasn't bad behavior. With careful thought, she considered that curling up in a ball was Cathie's way of demonstrating that their confrontational interactions overwhelmed her. She was stressed far beyond her capabilities and came up with this last resort for calming down. Maybe crouching down, arms around her bent knees with head down, holding herself still in one contained posture actually did calm Cathie down. She needed to be physically held in one place. And if Lia wasn't offering to do this, Cathie would do it herself. Lia felt forlorn thinking all this over. She hadn't been there for Cathie in the way she'd needed her to be. Her earlier assumption that Cathie was just trying to get out of doing homework was abandoned. Lia also realized that Cathie was regulating her body and settling her mind by being in a small, quiet place.

So the next day, when Cathie repeated the behavior of running around instead of completing her work, Lia got quiet and waited. Lia's pausing settled Cathie down somewhat, but she was obviously still overwhelmed and she slumped down to the floor, assuming the same crouched position she'd been in the day before. Lia sat with her. This was a dramatic change; Lia's frustration wasn't escalating Cathie's overstimulation.

With her hands gripped tightly and head down in shame, Cathie said meekly, "I hate that I can't do things right. I feel so stupid."

"I know," Lia replied in a hushed voice, "but there is no one right way to do things, even homework. We'll figure things out."

After a few minutes of sitting together on the floor, Cathie returned to the table and did a little more work. By refraining from quick action, Lia noticed that the issue shifted from the homework to Cathie's self-esteem and being emotionally overwhelmed. That became the priority. Cathie's high level of activity, overstimulation, and anxiety were powerful. Being angry at Cathie and giving her orders the other day had made it even harder for her to cope with her self-image, which increased the loss of her equilibrium. Lia's ability to step back led her to a different point of view. A new parenting mindset was taking hold. She recognized Cathie needed her emotional support before anything else could be accomplished.

STEP TWO
Self-Reflecting

Later that night, Lia sat with Dale at the computer so he could read about the five steps to Parental Intelligence. She told him how she had stepped back and, just with that one initiative, had begun to understand what Cathie was going through. Dale could see a big shift in his wife's attitude. Lia also understood better what she herself was going through. She explained that although she had to help Cathie do her homework, she would only be able to do that if she could strengthen their relationship by increasing Cathie's self-esteem. She felt she had to help Cathie cope with the idea of having ADHD because it made her feel so incompetent and ashamed. She told Dale that she hoped she might be able to support Cathie so Cathie could learn it wasn't her fault that she was disorganized and impulsive.

Dale read about the second step: self-reflecting. He expressed his pain in seeing Cathie struggle and thought they should try to recall what it was like to be in elementary school to get a sense of what Cathy might be going through. Dale remembered how powerful parents and teachers seemed to him and how, as a child, he worried about meeting their standards. He thought back to how he felt when he wasn't smart enough or at the top of his class. Maybe his own experiences had helped him feel empathy with Cathie's struggles, which made him refrain from pushing her to finish her work. He didn't think this was a solution because he wasn't helping Cathie complete her assignments, but at least it clarified why he held back.

Lia had been a more successful student. She remembered how her peers looked up to her academically, though she was rather awkward socially. Those memories helped her understand more fully how being socially out of the loop must feel to Cathie. Although Cathie was well liked, her learning difficulties made her feel different. Lia told Dale she wanted to find a way to let Cathie know that she wasn't less of a person because she had ADHD. With these beginning reflections out in the open, they felt more ready to face the obstacles in Cathie's way and to become the parents she needed. Cathie needed to know they were on her side, not just trying to change her.

They thought about what Cathie had said about feeling stupid and embarrassed when she left the classroom to go for reading help. Dale thought that would have crushed him when he was her age. Lia agreed that was painful for Cathie and felt they had to intervene quickly because her self-esteem was dwindling rapidly. These thoughts took them further back to their childhoods, when specific adults supported them.

Because Lia was socially awkward, one of her teachers used to eat lunch with her in the classroom. She, in turn, helped the teacher with the bulletin board, which made her feel important. Then the teacher would go with her into the schoolyard and stand there while Lia ventured forth to talk and play with other children. Knowing the teacher was standing there gave her courage. Lia wanted to be like that teacher for Cathie.

Dale reflected on his pain at having trouble with his studies. He didn't have ADHD, but he had learning disabilities. Although he had become a successful businessman, he was still slow at reading and much better with numbers. No one knew about learning disabilities when he was a boy, so his peers just called him "stupid"—which is the way Cathie felt. Only in high school did his self-esteem grow because he was an outstanding athlete. He was treated like a leader on the field, and the coach praised him a great deal. He never forgot this coach. When he went to college, he played college football and was given special help with his learning disabilities. The combination served him well. His self-esteem became more stable.

Reflecting together on their past experiences helped Lia and Dale see Cathie's struggles more clearly. They set about to find ways to help her with the problem that was central to all her struggles—low self-image.

STEP THREE
Understanding Your Child's Mind

Cathie trusted her mother, even though they battled. She felt relieved after her mother told her there was no one right way to do things. She believed her mother wanted the best for her, so when she had a problem with a friend, she went to her mother to discuss it.

"Mommy, Darla has been ignoring me on the playground at recess. I don't know why. I don't think I did anything to upset her. But she often talks behind other people's backs, and I'm afraid she's doing that now and the whole group is going to start ignoring me. She's been mean to other girls by making things up about them, but she's never been mean to me. Now it's my turn. I don't know why she's so popular, but the girls listen to her."

Lia thought this was a good opportunity to try to understand Lia's thoughts and feelings. She believed that, with some support, Cathie could handle this problem. Lia was able to hold her daughter's mind in mind as she encouraged Cathie to prepare herself before speaking to her friend. She told Cathie she was smart to think through this situation with her unpredictable friend rather than just reacting quickly. She empathized with Cathie's hurt and surprise at being ignored and told her she was sure Cathie could deal with this problem. Her mother's belief in Cathie gave her not only a feeling of being understood but also more faith in herself. Lia didn't take over and tell Cathie what to do. Instead, she shored up her confidence—the overarching problem.

Cathie decided to face the other eight-year-old when she could get her alone. While she didn't feel strong academically, her conversation with her mother had strengthened her sense of self in social relationships, where she was readily accepted. One afternoon, Cathie summoned up her courage to boldly ask Darla why she was ignoring her. She surprised Darla with her directness and caught her off guard. In this one-to-one situation, without her group behind her, Darla apologized, and Cathie felt relieved and even triumphant.

The homework situation was more difficult because Lia needed to understand the mind of her child in light of her ADHD. She had to imagine herself in Cathie's hyperactive world. Lia was a calm person generally, so she had no experiences with her body feeling out of control, and she had never struggled with focusing or concentrating. One Saturday, when Cathie was on her medicine, Lia decided to ask Cathie to describe her experience when she was off her medicine. She encouraged Cathie by telling her she promised she was not critical of her, but really wanted to be on her side by knowing what she was going through.

"Mommy, what does *deficit* mean?" Cathie asked. "I don't think I like that word."

Lia was surprised by that question, so she tried to respond carefully, not wanting to hurt her daughter. "Let's figure that out together. *Deficit* means that you don't quite have enough of something some of the time, even though you have it other times. For example, do you have trouble paying enough attention to my directions sometimes when you are off the medicine here at home, but when you are on the medicine, it is easier to pay attention to the teacher's directions at school?"

"Oh," Cathie said in a quiet voice. "It does happen at school, too, even with the medicine. The teacher tells me to stop talking and pay attention. I forget to keep listening when she says do this and that and this and that. She says too many things. I can't remember them all. I forget to keep listening and talk to my friend. She doesn't like that."

"That sounds difficult," Lia said sympathetically. "How do you feel when she says not to talk to your friends?" Lia asked.

"Embarrassed. I don't mean to do it," Cathie said. "It just happens. I'll try harder, Mommy."

"I know you don't do it on purpose. We can think of how to work that out when I understand even better. Sometimes you like to run around during your homework. What do you feel like inside at those times?" Lia asked gently.

"Well, sometimes I don't have an 'off' button. I can't stop myself from moving around. Sometimes it's scary. In the morning, I wake up feeling all jumbled up inside. I don't like how it feels. That's why I'm glad to take the medicine. Then that jumbled feeling goes away. "Also," Cathie continued, "the medicine makes it easier for me to concentrate in school. Then I don't feel I'm bad and don't blurt out stupid things like I used to in second grade."

Cathie was so glad to have this chance to tell her mother what had been happening inside of her. She continued at a rapid pace, unloading what she'd kept to herself for a long time.

"Sometimes when I'm talking to my friends and having fun, I forget what I'm saying. It's like in the middle of a sentence my mind jumps to something else. The kids don't notice. It's when I'm hyper."

"Hyper?" Lia asked.

"Yes, you know. *Hyper.* Like I said before, jumbled up. It used to be much worse. The medicine helps a lot," Cathie explained, pleased her mother was so receptive. "Oh, and another thing. This is funny. I lose things and find them in funny places later. Like, the other day, you told me to put my shoes on to get ready for the bus because I was late. Yeah, I know I lose track of time. It just gets later before I know it and I was really trying to rush, but I couldn't find one of the sneakers in my room. I went in the bathroom to brush my hair—I know it's messy, sorry—and my other shoe was in the bathroom. I don't know how it got there!"

"That is funny," said Lia. But she didn't mean it; it was sad. Hearing Cathie unleash so many thoughts and feelings about her ADHD muddled Lia's mind. Lia felt a wave of anxiety just trying to keep up with all that her daughter was pouring out. She was finally imagining what it might feel like to be in Cathie's jumbled world. How could she help her sort things out so every day wasn't such an upward battle? She had a lot to think about. And to think she used to scold Cathie on top of all this. Her daughter had been carrying a mighty load all by herself.

Later that evening, Lia shared their conversation with Dale. It broke his heart to hear all the details. However, he was immensely pleased that Cathie and Lia were developing such an open relationship. Clearly, Cathie trusted Lia, who had relieved her daughter of a heavy burden.

Lia took a different tack the next time the homework situation arose, although this time, Cathie actually got overwhelmed more quickly. In only a few minutes after starting her homework, Cathie was under the table.

"Cathie, how ya doing down there?"

"I'm scared," Cathie whispered.

"Oh dear. What are you scared of? I'm right here with you." Lia sat on the floor near her.

"I'm scared that I'm bad and stupid."

"You're not bad or stupid. I know homework is hard to do when you're off your medicine. I bet under the table is a special place for you to calm down."

"I'm coming out now. I'll try to finish the sentences."

This exchange shows that Lia was beginning to understand her daughter's mind. She was looking at her little girl's physical reactions as part of a dialogue with her. Running around meant she couldn't contain her hyperactivity and was upset by it. Hiding under the table was an attempt to reduce the inner stimulation she couldn't handle. Recognizing there was "physical dialogue," Cathie's mother was getting in touch with many aspects of her daughter's experience. Cathie, in turn, valued this new contact with her mother. Their mother-daughter relationship was growing.

STEP FOUR
Understanding Your Child's Development

Lia and Dale knew that it was hard for Cathie to keep up with the demands of a third grader. She struggled to stay organized, read at grade level, and follow directions. While most girls her age were developing longer attention spans, this was the heart of Cathie's struggle in school. She was easily distracted and chatted too easily with other children who were trying to do their classwork. Her distraction also contributed to her poor reading comprehension. She lost her place while reading and couldn't focus on the story line. In math, she seemed to concentrate better, but Lia and Dale knew they had to keep an eye on her work as the mathematics became more difficult. Lia and Dale realized that they needed to learn more about ADHD so they could help their daughter tolerate frustration more effectively. They knew she lost her equilibrium easily, like a much younger child. They also knew Cathie measured herself against her peers academically. She endured a harsh sense of internal disapproval, which they needed to counteract to ease her shame and self-doubt.

However, they also recognized that Cathie's development was uneven. In other ways, she excelled. After Lia's discussion with Cathie about being ignored on the playground, she felt Cathie was ahead of many girls in her ability to be compassionate. Dale felt that, with his wife's help, Cathie was developing a sense of who she was and how she wanted to be perceived as a friend. He also felt she was learning to think ahead to solve problems and set goals for herself.

Lia and Dale promised each other to focus on Cathie's strengths as well as her troubles. If they only saw problems when they looked at Cathie, then that was how she would look at herself. It was time to help their child be reminded of her unusual strengths, her kindness and generosity, her good humor and openness—all good qualities Cathie had internalized. They were proud of her growing moral sense, which she had developed at home and at church. Cathie needed to hear from them very specifically what made them proud.

STEP FIVE
Problem Solving

Lia decided to talk to Cathie about plans that would strengthen Cathie's ability to tolerate frustration as well as soothe herself when experiencing that frustration. She also wanted her daughter to have more fun, and together they discussed ways to do just that.

"Cathie, I know it's hard having a long day at school and then coming home to more work. How can we make after-school times better for you?"

"Okay," Cathie responded. "I'd like to have more time with my friends. I like them, and I also want to go to their dance school with them. I think I'd make a good dancer."

"I think playdates are a great idea," Lia said. "But I think we should limit them to one day a week after school. You'll have plenty of time to see your friends on the weekend. Then on a second afternoon, you can join the dance school. We'll get you the clothes you need. I'll call the dance school tomorrow and see what openings they have. Get a piece of paper and we'll make a list of the friends you'd like to invite to a playdate."

As Cathie tore a piece of paper from her notebook, Lia continued, "There's also a Boys & Girls Club at the church. They meet every other Sunday afternoon following Sunday school. Would you like me to sign you up for that?"

"Okay!" Cathie exclaimed. "I heard about that group. They go on trips together and make arts and crafts and play games."

Cathie was enjoying her mother's enthusiasm. Talking to her mother was getting to be easy—so much better than the arguments they used to have.

Lia was glad that Cathie was involved in problem solving. She was learning how social Cathie wanted to be. Having play dates would push homework to later in the day or evening, so that would still have to be worked out, but she'd be happier when it came time to do it. Also, the dance class was a great idea for Cathie's self-esteem. It was social and athletic. She remembered how her husband's self-esteem soared as an athlete. But they certainly didn't have to wait for Cathie to enter high school to give her something to be proud of.

Homework was still a daily problem to solve. Lia learned that recurrent problems do not have to be solved all in one day. As far as their imaginations would allow, they could keep coming up with ideas to explore and try. Lia sought support groups and professional help to find out various options for helping her daughter so she would be giving her the best possible care.

One particular afternoon, Cathie and her mother came up with a new plan for doing homework.

"Cathie, let's see if we can make a plan for your homework so we don't get mad at each other anymore. Do you have any ideas?" Lia asked.

Cathie appeared solemn and replied thoughtfully, "I can only do a little bit at a time, then I need to play or run around a little bit. When I feel all hyper inside, I can't concentrate. Mommy, I really want you to understand that, so you don't get mad. When you get mad, I get more hyper inside and it gets worse."

Lia was grateful for Cathie's honesty. She was surprised that she didn't even feel hurt. "I won't get mad anymore. I'll try really hard. I know you're right. We're learning together. The idea of doing only some work at a time would be good for both of us. You know what I'm going to do? I'm going to get that Little Mermaid clock from your room. What would you think of having a clock right with us?"

Cathie looked at her quizzically. "What's the clock for?"

"You could work for ten minutes, then you could do what you want for another five minutes. You could check the clock and do your work for another ten minutes, followed by a snack. Before we know it, the twenty minutes of homework will be finished and you can play."

"I can try that. I think I can sit for ten minutes at a time if I know I get a break in between," agreed Cathie, warming up to the idea. "I like the timing rule. I can do that."

Seeing her daughter's attentive face after months of frustration, Lia realized that this was a moment to hold on to. Maybe she'd call her mother in France to see if she'd fly in for a visit. Cathie was wearing the blue sweater Lia's mother had sent her. She should see her in it. Lia knew she'd been hesitant to invite her for months because she felt she wouldn't approve of either her granddaughter's behavior or her mothering. Lia's mother never yelled. She had pictured her mother's face blanching at the sight of Cathie's messy eating habits at dinner—she expected three courses! And she shrunk back at the thought of her mother chastising her for ever threatening anything, much less no dessert—an essential part of a French meal.

But Lia was feeling differently now. It was time for her to grow up and no longer feel she was living by her mother's rules. There was no end to self-reflection. She was Cathie's mother and knew what she was doing. Maybe that's why she had been so frustrated with Cathie—because deep down, she thought her own mother would disapprove. What a mistake that was. Cathie was under the pressure of two generations of mothers! Thinking more clearly now, Lia realized she had actually been underestimating her mother's capacities like she'd been underestimating her own and Cathie's. Her mother adapted to American ways the few times she had been here. She would just have to adapt to Cathie's struggles and try to understand them. Even her mother should be given the chance to grow. It had been too long since her mother had seen her animated granddaughter, and Lia wanted her to get to know Cathie better. After all, Cathie was just another version of their line of generally good-natured females.

Placing her hands on Cathie's round shoulders, she looked at her closely, as if seeking permission to continue. Cathie returned her gaze, eyes brightly anticipating her mother's next remark. Reassured by her daughter's receptive look, Lia said, "Your teacher is so pleased with your enthusiasm lately. She found out from a special committee that she can arrange for you to get less homework than the other children, just enough to show you understand the reading and math. Your teacher is a kind lady. She likes you, Cathie. Don't forget that."

In the coming weeks, problem solving with her mother worked well for Cathie, not only with her homework, but with building her self-esteem, too. Mother and daughter were getting along much better now. Threats and yelling seemed to be a thing of the past. Being engaged with each other in this new way opened new doors. Together, they came up with variations for doing homework such as doing different sections at different times of the night as well as in the early morning. Their planning had become flexible and creative. Problems were now viewed as opportunities for solving dilemmas that arose and new occasions for listening to each other.

In addition to having less homework than the other students, Cathie was given extended time for classwork, permission to leave the classroom when overwhelmed, and time with her teacher to go over any information missed due to impaired concentration. Problem solving was a new skill that enriched Cathie's coping mechanisms, helped her tolerate more frustration, and brought her closer to Lia. But it wasn't only Cathie who needed ongoing support; her parents did, too. Lia kept in contact with the ADHD blogger mothers, and Dale joined her at a monthly support group for parents.

The commotion at home didn't stop completely, but the dramatic scenes were over. This Nebraska front-porch home had become happy again. Lia, Dale, and Cathie were learning together, spending more time smiling and laughing, and far less time feeling unhinged and confused. The overall problem, Cathie's self-esteem, had taken priority. Their world was well again; they could count on each other. Mother, father, and daughter were all on the same side.

Chapter Nine

A Mother's Angst

Thirteen-Year-Old Olivia

Five-foot-two Olivia was a feisty, athletic teen who did average work in middle school. She lived in southern Illinois in the town where her parents, Delia and Cal, had grown up and gone to college. They had met in high school, went to the local liberal arts college, and married soon after graduation. They both earned their doctorates in sociology from schools back East, and then returned to their hometown to raise a family. Both parents became professors at the local college. When Olivia was born, her mother, Delia, reduced her hours and worked part-time so she could be home, while her father, Cal, increased his evening teaching hours.

By the time Olivia was thirteen, she had her own thoughts about her future. She wanted to leave her hometown to explore more of the world. She didn't want to duplicate her parents' life and raise her own family in the town where she was born. Through Facebook, she was in contact with girls around the country. She especially liked seeing their photos: how they dressed, what interested them, places they went. She studied their pictures for hours and lived for their emails. She took her laptop to bed and always quickly replied to comments and messages, hoping she was making friends in distant places. Because New York and California seemed exciting and unfamiliar, she was especially drawn to girls who lived in those places.

Olivia's mother and father had a close bond and tried to parent Olivia together, though her mother made most decisions about Olivia's daily life because her husband worked long hours, often coming home after eight o'clock. Together, they monitored Olivia's grades and encouraged her extracurricular activities. A terrific lacrosse and soccer player, Olivia was outgoing and had many friends because she was not only fun, but also trustworthy—a true-blue confidante. An independent soul since preschool, she had an easy time separating from her mother and finding her own way. She stood up for herself with peers and was always surrounded by "the crowd." Despite this, her sense of self was marred by her academic difficulties.

Unlike her daughter, Delia was serious and prone to worrying. She had trouble understanding that Olivia's self-esteem was built on her relationships. Due to her own general mistrust of others, she often misinterpreted Olivia's eagerness to be with friends and feared unnecessarily that Olivia's social involvement was potentially risky. She wished her husband was more available because his steadiness balanced her fearfulness. Unlike her daughter, Delia didn't have close friends with whom she could share her concerns. Having limited emotional resources, she nearly always reacted quickly, her anxieties forging rash decisions about Olivia's social life. She gave her a strict early curfew, wouldn't allow her to wear makeup, and picked out her clothes—outfits that wouldn't reveal Olivia's growing female shape. She believed she was doing her duty as a mother by keeping a close eye on how her daughter dressed and where she went.

Olivia's teacher scheduled a trip to Washington, DC. Delia's immediate worry was whether Olivia should be staying so far away from home in a hotel with boys. Without consulting her daughter, she called the teacher to see if she could be a chaperone, but was told all the chaperones had already been selected. Olivia had been very excited to be going off on her own, but when she learned her mother had made the call, she felt embarrassed, even furious.

"Mommy, my teacher told me you offered to be a chaperone. You should have asked me first," Olivia complained, feeling her mother had overstepped her bounds, as she had so often before.

"Perhaps," Delia responded, trying to sound more certain than she felt. "But you are too young to be going that far away and staying with boys in a hotel where—"

"Mommy!" Olivia interjected. "The boys will be nowhere near me."

"And where will the boys be?"

"They're on a floor above, and you should have—"

"There could be drugs and boys could sneak off their floor. How are you supposed to deal with that? Since I can't join you on the trip, you won't go either."

Olivia's eyes widened with disbelief. Even for her mother, this was ridiculous. "Mommy! You can't possibly mean that."

"I do mean it! And that's the end of it. If you bring it up again, you'll be grounded for a week."

Knowing her mother very well, Olivia could see how frightened her mother was, so she changed her tactics, hoping a more understanding approach would work better. "I know you get scared about things, but the school, my teachers planned this. They've been taking my grade on this trip for years. You can trust them to keep an eye on everyone."

Olivia's words fell on deaf ears. Delia had become the mother crocodile guarding her young from predators. She wasn't thinking about the way her actions were affecting Olivia, until Olivia said, "That's it. I'm running away. I'm getting out of this house."

Not that Olivia was actually going to run away, but Olivia's threat finally made Delia realize that her reaction to the school trip had been overly dramatic and unrealistic.

STEP ONE
Stepping Back

At an early age, Olivia became tuned into her mother's anxieties. For some children, such a fearful mother would create similar kinds of fears in the child. However, in this case, her mother's worrisome approach to life made Olivia become the calm and rational one in the relationship. Naturally, she began looking for ways she and her mother could interact about this school trip more sensibly.

In an email exchange with one of her new friends from New York, she was surprised to hear that this girl's mother also gave early curfews and didn't trust her daughter. So it wasn't just Midwestern mothers, after all. Here was a girl who understood. Olivia wrote to this girl about her own situation, and her online friend informed her that her mother was loosening up because she was reading about something called "Parental Intelligence" in an e-zine online. Her friend sent the link to Olivia, who forwarded it to her own mother, hoping that she'd give it more thought in an email than if she just told her about it. Then she waited for her mother to notice.

When Delia read Olivia's email, she found herself as curious as Olivia had hoped. Olivia had never written to her before, and Delia rarely used the Internet, except to buy things online, so this email communication from her daughter seemed to carry weight. She herself had never read an e-zine. The first article led to the next. What was Parental Intelligence? Did she have it? Could she learn it? There were five steps. She was intrigued.

Delia decided that she could certainly try the first one: stepping back. She owed Olivia that much. She knew Olivia was a great kid, a warm daughter who tried hard at everything she did. Delia also knew that when Olivia thought her mother was overreacting, her husband often agreed, though not in front of Olivia. So she'd step back and give this way of thinking a try.

Delia thought back to Olivia's announcement that her class was going to Washington, something they had all been looking forward to as part of their eighth grade experience. Olivia's mother knew that it was a rite of passage in her community, though she wasn't thinking that when she'd said no. She recalled Olivia's excitement about staying in a hotel room with her friends. It was important to Olivia to fit in with and belong to a group. Upon reflection, Delia realized that she had foreclosed what could have been an intimate discussion with her daughter about new adventures with friends. She realized that thoughts about Olivia being without her in another city revived her own fears of drugs and sex at the same age. This understanding caused her to question why and how she had lost her balance over this school trip. However, at the thought of wavering on her decision, Delia still felt a sense of foreboding; when those emotions returned, her fear of exposing Olivia to drugs and sex returned, too. But she asked herself if she had missed a chance to get to know Olivia better and find out what she was going through. She had a PhD in sociology, but when it came to her daughter, she forgot everything she knew. She just became frightened.

Delia wanted to find a way to reopen their discussion. Slowing down her thoughts helped her to realize that calling the teacher so precipitously excluded Olivia from the decision-making process and embarrassed her. Stepping back led her to think there were many more options for figuring out the best way to handle the situation. As she mentally replayed the whole discussion in slow motion, she remembered Olivia's anticipation of traveling away from home to visit a new city. Through her daughter's eyes, she saw the wonder and joy of growing up. She thought about how she had tried to protect Olivia with strict curfews, restricted TV, and added parental controls on her computer. She realized that she often presumed the worst and made assumptions about Olivia that weren't warranted. She asked so many questions about Olivia's friends because she worried about bad influences. She asked herself, *Am I trying so hard to protect Olivia that I am acting like a warden instead of a loving mother?*

Delia was reminded of an incident that occurred when Olivia was eleven. Olivia had drawn a fake tattoo on her wrist, a heart with the name of the boy she liked that day. Unfortunately, Olivia used ink that didn't readily come off when that boy was out of the picture. Olivia cried her eyes out, fearing she'd be embarrassed forever. At that time, Delia intuitively stepped back and stayed with Olivia throughout her tears. She listened to her fears of humiliation. Eventually, they found a cleanser that removed most of it, leaving the rest to wear off on its own. But Olivia felt comforted, not chastised or embarrassed. Delia realized she had a different parenting mindset then. What had happened? Somehow a fake tattoo didn't scare her as much as going away to Washington. The e-zine spoke about self-reflecting. It did seem to be the next natural step. What was she so intensely worried about? She knew she better figure it out before talking to Olivia about the trip again or she'd just get those threatening feelings back and mess things up.

STEP TWO
Self-Reflecting

Delia overheard Olivia asking a friend on the phone if she was seeing anyone. When the other girl apparently asked her as well, Olivia admitted she had never had a date and didn't think she was very pretty and thought she was kind of ordinary looking. Delia knew she was eavesdropping and walked away guiltily, but she was surprised Olivia didn't find herself appealing to boys. She was particularly struck by the word "ordinary." It wasn't that Delia wanted Olivia to start dating at thirteen—she definitely didn't—but she did not want her daughter to think of herself as unattractive, either. She was taken aback, even hurt on her daughter's behalf. What did Olivia actually see when she looked in the mirror? Had she contributed to Olivia's view that she was ordinary by the clothes she chose for her because she was so afraid of how boys might view her?

Delia remembered looking in the mirror for long periods of time when she was Olivia's age. She'd brush her thick, curly hair in different styles. She'd never seen Olivia do that. She dressed quickly and ran off to school. She acted as if athletes didn't care about those things. She never argued about the no-makeup rule. But to her friend, she revealed she didn't think she was pretty. Delia realized that Olivia did care about those things after all, but she tried to hide those feeling from her mother.

Delia knew she had been an anxious child, but she never saw Olivia that way. Her daughter was not anxious; she was adventurous. Was questioning her attractiveness just a typical behavior at age thirteen? Delia was not sure. Hearing her daughter describe herself as unattractive added another layer of anxiety to her current worries about the Washington trip, but Delia knew that her present anxiety had nothing to do with Olivia's struggles. *I have my own personal supply of fears,* she thought, *and Olivia is being hurt by them. I've been thinking of the boys in her grade as potential intruders into her hotel room. That's beyond reason.*

Delia considered going to a late-afternoon movie, a comedy at the local theater, to get her mind off things for a while. But the thought of being alone in the theater made her uneasy. Being a woman alone in a dark place made her shudder; she thought she'd feel strangely self-conscious sitting alone. Suddenly, she wanted to hide in her bedroom; clearly, her anxiety was out of hand. She made a cup of tea and called Cal, but he wasn't in his office.

It was while sipping her tea that she suddenly realized the source of her fears about Olivia. For years, she had fought thinking about this, but her recent struggles with her daughter forced her to revisit the time when she was raped in a park by a boy on drugs. She was thirteen. She went home and told her parents, and they immediately contacted the police. The boy was never caught. Her parents found it difficult to talk about the rape; even making the police report had been difficult for them, so they simply stopped talking about it. They may have felt that the consequences of the rape were over, but Delia cried for nights on end and at times woke up dreaming she was screaming for help, only to realize she was just whispering. Her distant parents didn't pick up the signals of what became a deep emotional problem for her.

Her parents never understood the aftermath of the rape, but Delia wanted to be a better parent for Olivia. She recalled that during the discussions about the trip, Olivia had mentioned that she knew her mother had fears. Delia suddenly realized that Olivia often gave up her own needs in order to calm her mother down. Delia wondered if Olivia held her in contempt because of this, a feeling strengthened by her tone of voice. Maybe this was why Olivia didn't trust her with her concerns about her appearance. Delia recalled her own hidden contempt for her mother because she never understood that her nighttime distress needed attention. She had told her mother about her nightmares, but her mother just said they'd go away. Her mother was blind. Delia sadly recalled that her mother seemed to give more attention to her own needs than caring for a daughter who had been raped. Delia wondered if she was doing the same thing with Olivia; if she was so protective, not of Olivia, but of herself.

Delia desperately wanted her husband to stabilize her fears, but more often than not, he was unavailable. He meant well, but he wasn't there when she needed him. She knew she had to come to terms with her past on her own because it was hurting her daughter. She was as wary of help as she was frantic about needing it, but she finally decided she would seek out treatment for her anxiety. She knew psychotherapy would take much time, however, and she had to be emotionally available to Olivia right now, before she could reconcile her own past. She was lucky to find a psychotherapist who was familiar with Parental Intelligence.

The therapist suggested that Delia not only focus on her own past pain but also on Olivia's mind. Delia knew that Olivia thought she was treating the trip like a crisis. She didn't know, however, that this was not only tremendously disappointing to Olivia, but also that her daughter found her mother's actions strange.

STEP THREE
Understanding Your Child's Mind

Delia was thinking about how, fifteen years earlier, she and Cal had settled in their hometown to start their family. They used to talk about their idea of the picture-perfect life: professors at their alma mater; a healthy, cheerful baby; and a marriage that lasted forever. Now, circumstances—her own past, as well as Olivia's increasing need for independence—were beginning to slowly dismantle that dream. Her baby had become a child with youthful exuberance. She was clearly a can-do kid, maturing into an empathic, delightful teenager with everything she needed to be happy—except that her mother seemed to drag her down. Delia feared that Olivia looked at her with doubt, knowing that anxiety affected her judgments. Since her thirteenth birthday, Olivia had begun to openly question her mother's decisions about her social life. The Washington trip was a case in point—the last straw, as it were—and Delia felt an emotional void growing between them.

Delia noticed that Olivia was becoming increasingly wary when around her. She caught her daughter glancing at her as if expecting the next odd behavior or decision. Delia was becoming self-conscious because she sensed that her nervous behaviors were noticeable and affected her daughter. Delia was aware she was having more and more trouble masking her emotions. She noticed Olivia shaking her head when she heard her mother talking about the trip with her father on the phone. Delia was beginning to realize that Olivia saw her reactions about the trip as a betrayal. Was it?

Delia was relieved to be in therapy with someone who could help her improve her relationship with her daughter. She didn't want Olivia to continue to hold her at arm's length. After just two therapy sessions and a talk with her husband, Delia recognized remorsefully that the prospect of the Washington trip with boys and girls in the same hotel had triggered memories of her rape. She had reacted as if Olivia was in actual danger.

She clearly knew now she had reacted hastily and harshly without giving thought to Olivia's needs. As a result, she had surrendered some of her authority as a parent because her judgment had become questionable. Olivia's old view of her mother as a role model with a high standing in the college and the community had vanished, at least for the time being. But Delia was plagued most by the fact that witnessing her anxiety meant that Olivia recognized that her mother was flawed, resulting in a loss of her childlike innocence. Olivia may have been aware of her mother's excessive worries prior to the discussion about the trip, but now it was blatant. She felt transparent in front of her daughter, even though Olivia knew nothing about the trauma she had suffered as a teen. She had to address the trip with Olivia, reverse her decision, and apologize without burdening her any further.

With her husband's help, Delia apologized for her swift decision, and Olivia did go to Washington. However, a palpable distance had established itself between mother and daughter. Olivia barely spoke to her. After describing the situation to her therapist, Delia realized that she might be making Olivia feel emotionally isolated at home the way she herself had felt with her own mother after her rape.

With that in mind, Delia sensed that Olivia was tired of her mother falling apart easily with unnecessary worries, and therefore had stopped telling her about her friends and weekend plans.

Certainly, Olivia was distancing herself from her mother. When asked where she was going, she'd respond curtly, and she even stopped asking for rides, relying on her friends' parents or her father to take her places instead. Tolerating this emotional distance was difficult for Delia. She missed their casual conversations.

Delia became more determined than ever to try to be cognizant of what was on Olivia's mind. She knew her style of relating to Olivia needed to change quickly and that she should listen more attentively to whatever she said without displaying her own immediate emotions. Deciding to put Olivia's feelings ahead of her own was long overdue. The way her emotions had interfered with her daughter's life would elude Delia no longer.

STEP FOUR
Understanding Your Child's Development

In addition to considerations about Olivia's emotional development, Delia also needed to think further about her physical development. Olivia's body had been changing rapidly. Her tight, athletic figure was becoming more shapely, and shopping together could be common ground for future interactions. Delia was aware that Olivia wanted more privacy and autonomy. When Delia realized that Olivia was taking care of her, she saw that the mother-child roles had been reversed. She addressed this directly by telling Olivia that her anxiety was in control and that it was not Olivia's job to alleviate it.

Olivia was surprised and visibly relieved that her mother discussed this with her openly. It helped her feel her mother was being a parent again, an adult looking out for her child's best interests.

Delia also told Olivia how proud she was of her for going to Washington so confidently. She had grown as a parent since the calamity about Washington and now recognized that Olivia's distancing was a clue to the psychological separation her daughter needed at this time in her life. Olivia was not just attempting to skirt her mother's supervision and variable emotional state. Delia recognized that Olivia needed a mother who was supportive of her wish to grow up, a mother who could foster her own feminine self-esteem.

STEP FIVE
Problem Solving

Olivia made new friends on the Washington trip. She liked her roommates, but she branched out by visiting monuments and museums with others. One new friend was a boy named Carver, who was particularly adept at discussing art, something she knew little about. They spent a lot of time at the National Museum, and Carver enchanted Olivia with his knowledge and passion about paintings. She secretly hoped they might become more than just friends.

Olivia returned from Washington feeling good about herself, not only because she had met Carver, but also because she had felt liberated from her anxious mother. Once home, her sense of separation from her mother reasserted itself and restricted her from sharing stories about the trip.

But through her own efforts, Delia was proving to be more relaxed and approachable, and Olivia eventually felt she could tell her mother about Carver: his interest in art, how handsome he was, and how friendly he had been to her. She shared how proud she felt that someone so intelligent could be interested in her. She felt for the first time that she could be with the smart kids socially, if not in their classes.

Delia had been monitoring her own emotions carefully when with Olivia, but this new story about Carver caught her by surprise. She knew her experience of feeling included with the smart kids was a boon to her self-esteem, and she was glad for her. But suddenly, her old fears that this new acquaintance might lead to a boyfriend-girlfriend relationship frightened her: Olivia was only thirteen. However, upon reflection, even though she thought this was a reasonable concern, she didn't want to overreact, especially since nothing had happened except museum visits. She knew it would help to include her husband in this discussion, but he was away at a conference that week. She felt a sense of abandonment by him with his late hours and conferences and thought Olivia might feel this as well. However, she felt empowered by her therapist's support and thought she could take matters into her own hands.

That night, Delia asked Olivia if she would like to go shopping the next day for new spring clothes and go out to dinner later at the sushi restaurant in the next town. Olivia readily agreed. She was proud of her mother for wanting to do this because she knew her mother must have mixed feelings about Carver. Nevertheless, she sensed a new openness in her mother.

Delia tried to be less overbearing during their shopping trip. She let Olivia lead the way among the racks of clothes in the big department store where they usually shopped.

When Delia pointed out they weren't finding anything in the department store and suggested they drive to a little boutique in the next town instead, Olivia couldn't believe her ears. This boutique was written up in a fashion magazine one of the most popular girls in school, a friend of Carver's, had shown her. Olivia thought this was definitely a new side to her mother. Excited, she thought that maybe she'd get her mother to buy some new clothes for herself there, too.

In the car, Olivia was daydreaming about writing her friend in New York all about the boutique when Delia had to stop to allow for the passage of a long train. Olivia took out her phone and said, "Mommy, I put a lot of pictures on Facebook from the trip. Do you want to take a quick look while we're waiting?"

Delia found this to be an exciting moment because Olivia had never shared her Facebook page with her before. "Sure," she said, grinning.

"Here are pictures of my friends in the hotel room, but I have pictures of other kids, too. Here's a picture of Carver. Mommy, he's very smart and definitely cool."

"I can see why you're attracted to him, Olivia."

After the train gates went up, Olivia confessed, "I think he likes me."

Delia found it difficult to directly address her daughter's statement. She found herself skirting the issue. "It's hard to make new friends, Olivia, but you're so good at it," she responded.

At the boutique, Delia told Olivia they could continue looking at the pictures in the restaurant, and she climbed out of the car. Delia felt her interruption of Olivia's confession was abrupt and disconcerting, but she needed a moment to process the information and decide what to say.

In the boutique, Delia again let Olivia lead the way. Olivia tried on a dress and short boots, and when her mother saw her, she said with enthusiasm, "Let me tell you, kiddo, you look terrific. Carver should see you now!" Olivia was delighted that her mother not only liked the way she looked, but brought up Carver again. Earlier, she had doubted that her mother had really heard her comments about Carver in the car when she said she thought he liked her. Now she knew she had heard her after all.

"Mommy, why don't you buy something pretty to surprise Daddy?" Olivia asked. "He should notice you more. You are really pretty, and when I doubt myself, my friends tell me that I look like you."

Delia blushed. She was thrilled her daughter found her attractive and wanted to look like her. This was certainly new information. She was surprised the girls were complimenting Olivia by saying she looked like her. She thought they would only complain about their mothers. And "pretty"—that made her uneasy to know her daughter studied her attractiveness, but she couldn't overreact. Not now. Olivia was really opening up to her. What a remarkable child.

Olivia picked out a pair of skinny jeans for her mother and a floral, semisheer shirt. "Mommy, try this outfit on. It's not expensive, but it's definitely cool. Perfect for spring."

"Okay," said Delia, enjoying her daughter's mood. "I will!"

The jeans and shirt fit perfectly, and Delia caught an admiring expression on her daughter's face when they both looked in the mirror. To see her daughter admire her was all that she could hope for, a moment to savor. She had always wanted Olivia to admire her for her intelligence and her accomplishments, but this was something else; she was admiring her femininity. It felt magical, like a fantasy. Even if she didn't like the clothes, she would have bought them just to be connected to Olivia in this way.

Beautiful decorator shopping bags in hand, the pair headed back to the car. Delia thought her daughter's excitement would have peaked by now, but Olivia was still looking forward to the fancy sushi restaurant her mother had picked. She had so much to tell her New York friend.

They decided to share a large sushi and sashimi platter. When it came, the elaborate pattern of fish on a big wooden boat filled with radishes and ginger made them chuckle in delight. Over seaweed salad, Olivia said earnestly, "Mommy, I like Carver so much. We are friends now, but I think I want to be his girlfriend. I don't know if he wants to be my boyfriend, though."

Checking her natural concerns, Delia said that Carver sounded like a great guy. Olivia sensed uneasiness when her mother asked, "Olivia, how is it different being a girlfriend compared to being a friend?"

"I'm not really sure," she responded honestly. "But I think it's fun. You text every day and meet in between classes and at each other's lockers. Sometimes you go on Facebook and share pictures."

Olivia took out her phone and used the camera app to take a picture of the boat of sushi and sashimi. Delia burst out laughing. "Olivia, you just took a picture of our food!"

"Yeah, sure, when kids go to interesting places they put pictures on Facebook. Watch. I'll do it right now."

Delia found this little activity amusing and delightful. Olivia was sharing her life with her. She actually wanted her friends to see where her mother had taken her to dinner.

Olivia recognized that her mother was trying hard to communicate with her, and so she thought it the proper time to risk having a serious conversation about their relationship.

"Mommy, sometimes I worry about telling you things. I just told you about a boyfriend, and you haven't said much since. I think there's more you're not saying. You have that look on your face."

"I don't want you to think you have to take care of me," Delia responded.

"You're my mother. I should take care of you."

"Not at your own expense. But you seem to want me to be honest, so I will be. There could be more to the boyfriend-girlfriend thing than you imagine. It might lead to sex. You're only thirteen."

"You're right," Olivia replied. "I am thirteen. Sex. Ugh. Really? I'm not into that. Some girls talk about it, but I'm not there at all. Believe me. I've never had a date. I've never had a kiss. I'd probably tell you if I did."

She didn't have to tell me about Carver, Delia thought, *but she wanted to. Her trust in me is returning. I feel like I've got her back and don't want to lose her again. I see how this boy lifts her self-esteem. She can see she's not just an average kid with average grades; smart kids can like her, too. She's so terrific; there is really nothing about her that is average or ordinary—oh, I hate that awful word—ordinary. I hope I've disabused her of that feeling by taking her to the boutique. I must not spoil her fun.*

Olivia looked directly at her mother. "Mommy, why do you worry about sex? Tell me. I don't want you to worry about it. If I think you do, it makes me feel funny inside."

"Okay," said Delia without a plan of what she was going to say next. "Do you want to know about what it was like when I was your age?"

"Of course."

"When I was your age, most kids were alone after school, especially once they were in middle school. There was even a term for us: latchkey kids. We'd come home, let ourselves in, have a snack, and go out again. The town has changed since then, and parents are more involved with their children now. When both parents work today, they are texting their kids, hire someone to be at home, and know what their kids are doing. But when I was your age, we'd bike around all the time and go to the park. Parents didn't drive us, and your grandmother didn't really know where I'd go each day."

"Your parents didn't know where you went? That sounds strange. I guess Grandma trusted you a lot."

"She did," Delia whispered, "and I didn't do anything I shouldn't. But one day, a boy I didn't know jumped on me, and I got scared and ran home to tell my mother. After that, I became kind of a nervous kid. It was so unexpected. That's why I worry about you getting into situations that you might not be able to handle."

Delia did not want to say more. She didn't want to burden Olivia with the information that she had been raped at her age. She thought it was better to just explain her watchfulness over her daughter by simplifying the story. At that moment, she thought that if it felt like too much for her to tell about the rape, then it might also be too much to hear. For now, that was all she could do.

"That sounds awful," Olivia said. "I see now why you asked me about having a boyfriend and sex. I'm a lacrosse player. I'm strong and run fast. I can handle myself, Mommy, you can be sure of that. That was an awful experience for you. Thank you for confiding in me."

Delia's love for her daughter had fueled her determination to understand her own anxiety and not let it interfere with being a caring mother. She admired her daughter and had learned that her daughter trusted her. Delia was a complex woman who had started feeling anxious because of an unresolved memory, which dictated a poor decision about her daughter's school trip, but that wasn't all of her. Rebounding with the fortitude to look within herself revealed her courage and depth of character. She was learning about herself and her daughter and anticipating the promise of their deep and growing relationship.

Chapter Ten

A Messy Room Signals Depression

Fifteen-Year-Old Leslie

It was Saturday morning, and Leslie, an olive-faced and fit fifteen-year-old, was hiding out in her room. Leslie's parents divorced when she was six. Even though her father used to visit periodically for the first five years, she hadn't seen him much lately and missed him terribly. A handsome, charming man, though caring on the surface when he was with her, had proved unreliable over time. At first, she had hoped that she would forge a closer connection with him as she grew older, because, in her mind, he just wasn't good with little kids. But then, when she was nine, he remarried and had more children with his new wife. His new family kept him at an even greater distance. When she was eleven, he moved what Leslie called his "other family" across the country. Their only contact became occasional phone calls and ever-rarer visits. Although this was a tremendous blow and she grew doubtful that he still wanted a tie to her, her yearnings continued.

Ceci, Leslie's mother, was almost fifty. Slim, five-feet-eleven, with long, gray-tinged, curly hair, she usually dressed quite casually in torn jeans and a white tee. Her mornings were spent in the garden of their small house at the southern tip of the Florida Keys with a distant view of the ocean. Being a "farmer," as she put it, was her major relaxation. She spent most of her time in her studio, illustrating children's books for a living. She loved the work, but it kept her inside, and she reveled in the Key West sunshine when she took breaks from her storybook paintings.

On this particular Saturday, however, she felt no relaxation in her garden because she found herself worrying about her daughter. Over the past few months, Ceci had begun to notice some major changes in Leslie's behavior. Previously very tidy and organized, Leslie had become quite the opposite. Her bedroom was a mess. Ceci couldn't stop her ceaseless mind from thinking about her daughter, worried the change in behavior pointed to a deeper problem.

Later that day, Ceci stood in the kitchen, gripping a bouquet of flowers she'd just plucked but hadn't yet put into water. She'd walked into the house to do just that, but going down the hall had passed Leslie's wreck of a bedroom. She felt an unexplainable rage well up inside her. She couldn't decide whether to barge into Leslie's room to yell at her about the disorder she was living in or to proceed down the hall to her own room to just curl up on her bed from the emotional exhaustion that threatened to overpower her. Tossing the flowers she had cut from her garden into the kitchen sink, she abandoned both plans and fled into the living room, where she drew the curtains and lay on the sofa, looking up at the ceiling.

I have no idea how to handle the situation between Leslie and me, she thought, finding herself sobbing. *I'm so afraid she'll see my rage that I can't account for. I'm just so tired.*

Ceci recalled how she and Leslie used to talk endlessly. Leslie would confide in her about the things in her world that bothered her. She recollected one conversation from Leslie's first year of middle school as if it were yesterday:

"Mommy, I'm so ugly. I'm taller than all the other girls. I have boobs, and my friends are so skinny. Ugh!"

Ceci tried to console her. "It's hard to imagine, but being tall becomes wonderful when you are older. I know. I can wear anything and always look slim."

"Yeah. But I'm taller than Cole, and he's so nice. All the girls like him, but I don't have a chance."

"I know it's rough, honey. You seem so stressed, like something even more is bothering you."

"Oh, everything is changing!" Leslie cried. "I hate middle school. There are all these new kids from the three other elementary schools, and I feel like I'm losing my friends. All the friend groups are changing. I don't feel comfortable with my old group. They are splitting apart. I wish I was little again."

Lying on the couch in the darkened living room, Ceci recalled thinking that Leslie was too young to pine for earlier times. But she had set those thoughts aside, believing it was just the angst of being in middle school. *Maybe I was wrong,* Ceci continued to think, *because now Leslie has gone from being tidy to totally disorganized, and on top of that, she is beginning to do poorly in high school. That failing grade from a solid A+ student just doesn't make sense.* She wondered if Leslie even talked to her old best friend, Rava, anymore. Was she being just a defiant teenager, or was something tormenting her? Six months ago, she had taken away Leslie's cell phone for four weeks because she had lied about going to her friend's house when she actually went to a party with boys in the next town. Perhaps that was a mistake, because since then Leslie had stopped speaking to her at all.

Ceci remembered how, at first, Leslie became really curt and stopped confiding her feelings about things. That was so unusual. Remembering how close she had been with Leslie when she was in middle school, Ceci was saddened and felt like a bad mother; she didn't know her daughter anymore.

At the same time, Leslie slipped in and out of sleep in her room, wrapped in the brilliantly colored abstract quilt her mother had made for her. An all-too-familiar heavy sadness sank over her as she recalled her last dance recital when she was fourteen. It was the culmination of all her recitals because that time she was the star. It was a year ago, but it felt like no time had passed. She was on stage at the Partridge Theatre, only partly aware of her moving body, because she was wondering if her father was in the audience as he had promised. Even though he had broken so many promises, she still had secretly sent him a letter, inviting him to this special show where she was going to dance a solo accompanied only by a jazz quartet. He had responded, promising he would be there.

When the music stopped, it felt harsh. The clapping in the audience snapped her out of her reverie. She hardly remembered taking her bows before wheeling briskly off the stage with the other performers. Her mother hugged her affectionately in the noisy dressing room. She looked around one last time for her father, but of course, he was nowhere to be found. Her tense hopes that she could count on him had vanished. When dancing on stage, she had imagined that he was her adoring, admiring audience. Now, realizing he had never even shown up, a potent weight descended on her well-formed shoulders that had rotated only minutes before with the uplifting music. Despite her body's strength, it nearly gave out under the heavy weight of the towering disappointment she felt.

Waking from her daydream, Leslie returned to the present. That was her last recital; she had stopped dancing. She couldn't dance anymore. Her father's absence had felt too brutal, and the hip-hop rhythm didn't match her burgeoning downward spiral. She tried practicing after that performance, but the weight of his betrayal kept returning, and she couldn't dance anymore. His broken promise felt like a blatant lie, a final blow. The only way to relieve herself of this sense of violation was to give up dance. It worked for a while, but now, one year later, the weight returned to her shapely shoulders. Melancholy hung on her brow. She could feel her breathing slow as sleep showered over her, a gentle escape that eased the pain.

When she awoke, Leslie's thoughts turned to Craig, her boyfriend of four months, who had recently left her for another girl. She felt a pang of loss. At first, he had tried to get her to smoke weed with him, but she had refused. *Weed is so repulsive,* she thought. *I may have been a wreck, but I'm not a pothead. Why should I force myself to do things that aren't me?*

When Craig wasn't trying to get Leslie to use pot, she discovered there was much more to him. He was smart, and when he was not under the influence, he could really be there for her. Leslie found that he was a good listener; he knew what it was like to feel depressed, and they bonded over their feelings of loss. Craig used drugs to escape; Leslie used sleep. She'd told him about her father, and he was kind, so she told him all her secrets. It felt good to let them out. All the long hours of talking seemed so good for both teens, and Leslie thought Craig felt as close to her as she did to him. But then Val came into the picture, and Craig seemed to forget everything they had together. Val was an unusual person—brilliant, pretty, and daring—and Craig was taken with her. She was heavily into drugs, like Craig. Leslie might have helped him face things, but Val helped him escape, so he chose her.

I was so sad and even humiliated when he left, Leslie thought. *I was such an idiot for letting him into my life. I'm deleting all his pictures. I loved posting pictures of us together. It was like, if you didn't post a picture, you weren't even at the party. I was so into that. What a joke. Now that he's gone, the pictures mean nothing. It sucks. He was as confused as I was.*

Leslie felt lost but not defeated. She longed for her true girlfriends, whose texts she never returned, and for her devoted mother, her intimate protector, the one real person in her life who tried to know her better than she knew herself.

Mommy has been complaining about my messy room. Why don't I just straighten it out? And with that thought, she fell asleep.

STEP ONE
Stepping Back

Ceci remembered reading about Parental Intelligence. She'd used the five steps before, when Leslie was younger, and they'd helped her understand her reactions to Leslie, which prepared her better for future problems. *We always figured things out together,* Ceci thought. *Leslie be-*

came as introspective as I was and really began to think through what was going on in her mind. Why did I stop? I remember those five steps. Maybe stepping back would help.

Reaching back into her memories, Ceci's mind returned to planning Leslie's birthday when she was eight. She remembered balloons trailing at the mailbox, welcoming Leslie's nine girlfriends. The sun was shining lemon-yellow, covering the back garden. A large swing set, a jungle gym, and a trampoline filled one side of the yard, and a large picnic table filled the other. Ceci remembered how Leslie carefully extricated each girl's present from the pile. She didn't tear away the wrapping paper, but rather saved the pieces for her crafts. At eight, she knew what Canson Tientes pastel paper was, as well as Arches watercolor paper. She was a precocious artist who learned the tools of the trade, truly her artistic mother's daughter. And her friends knew her well. They had chipped in to buy an oak easel for her painting, and tank tops and neon colored leggings for her dancing. Leslie was so energetic and talented that she was both a hip-hop dancer and an artist. She danced two hours a day, four times a week at a dance school specializing in hip-hop.

As the girls played, Ceci sat to the side painting the scene with oil pastels. They loved being artists together, and Leslie was pleased when Ceci gave her the painting at the end of the day.

The memory of the party held Ceci for a long moment and then faded.

In the present again, Ceci tried to remember when Leslie stopped talking to her. *It had to be because of that punishment,* she thought. *It was hard for me to realize she'd lied to me. But I shouldn't have punished her. I guess I got scared. Panicked. Being a single parent can be difficult; I can give myself that. I lost my compass as a parent. We should have talked.*

STEP TWO
Self-Reflecting

Ceci decided to take the next step in Parental Intelligence: self-reflecting. What was happening to her at the moment she decided to punish Leslie instead of talking to her? Given she was sure that this was the tipping point that led Leslie to withdraw from her, she had to figure out her own thoughts and motivations if she was going to make any inroads with her daughter.

Ceci found herself thinking of her relationship with her own mother when she was Leslie's age. Leslie's detachment reminded her of her mother's long bouts with clinical depression, a situation that used to make her so angry. At fifteen, Ceci was forced to take care of her all-too-still, weeping mother. She sat by her side for long periods of time, trying to comfort her, but to no avail. She brought her tea and listened to her worries. All that time, it kept her away from her adventurous friends, whom she envied. She remembered having so many mixed feelings. While she felt guilty if she wasn't there for her mother, she yearned to be carefree going out with the other girls shopping, riding bikes, hanging out. She often felt she was missing out and was on the outside of things. She suddenly realized that her own memories of her mother had caused her present unaccountable rage to resurface. She was always there for her mother, but still deeply resented how it interfered with her teenage life. Wanting to forget this memory had blocked her from seeing that Leslie might be depressed. She hated to think what depression could do to someone. First her mother, and now her daughter?

STEP THREE
Understanding Your Child's Mind

Trembling with fear, Ceci had trouble holding onto the passing thought that Leslie's messy room might be a mirror of her mind. She knew that being grim wasn't characteristic of Leslie. Something was brewing. Her daughter was becoming self-absorbed. She seemed to be wrestling with something she couldn't sort out. Ceci couldn't quite get a handle on what was happening. She asked herself if she should try to talk to her. Would she listen?

Ceci recalled once again how Leslie used to be able to talk with her friend Rava when things weren't working out for either of them. They had a way of supporting each other and thinking things through. They relied on each other, even when their friend groups changed and they weren't in the same circles. Ceci thought if Leslie were depressed she might not even call on Rava. She had always been organized in her schoolwork and busy schedule; she and Rava were alike in that way. They admired each other's achievements. But if they weren't talking, Ceci didn't know if Leslie was even feeling pride in her accomplishments.

What am I missing? Ceci wondered. *Why was she so interested in the doped-up kids? What was she was running away from? By punishing her, I missed the meaning behind her behavior, and then she backed off from me because I didn't understand.*

Ceci's musings led her to another revelation: *I've been thinking so much about mothers that I've forgotten all about fathers. At least when I cared for my mother, my father was proud of me and thanked me. That buoyed my spirits back then. But Leslie doesn't have a father to boost her self-confidence. How could I have been so blind? Since her father moved away, I thought she was coping, but that's too simple. How could she possibly cope with his absence? It wasn't only his physical absence, but his emotional absence. They barely spoke. Oh my sweet child. The loss of my understanding only compounded the loss of his understanding. I have to help her address all this,* Ceci thought. *She must be feeling so alone.*

STEP FOUR
Understanding Your Child's Development

Ceci thought she should review more clearly Leslie's teenage development to make sure she was getting a clear read on things before she approached her. She always had lots of friends, but something changed after that party she punished her for. It wasn't only Rava. She had stopped contact with her other friends, as well. Instead, she spent a lot of time in her room, rarely leaving except to go to school. Ceci knew that teenagers often spent time in their rooms, on the phone, or on the computer, but she realized Leslie wasn't doing that. She found her sleeping a lot. The room was too quiet. Because they hadn't been talking, Ceci had no idea if Leslie was trying to get her grades back up after that one failing grade.

Shifting friend groups and detaching from her mother could be normal development for a teen like Leslie, but Ceci knew that losing confidence and withdrawing to such a great extent likely meant much more. Knowing that Leslie had always been self-reliant and motivated, Ceci's worries were escalating rapidly. She began to recognize even more fully how important a father was to a teenage girl. She thought about how girls longed for a father to admire them and build their self-image. Ceci's qualms heightened dramatically as her ideas crystallized: *Leslie needs to hear her father say that she's pretty and smart and special to him. My adoration isn't enough, and even that's been lacking lately.*

Suddenly, she gasped with what felt like an obvious revelation she had missed: *Leslie can't straighten up her room because she can't think straight!*

STEP FIVE
Problem Solving

Ceci ran upstairs and knocked on her daughter's door.

"Can I come in?"

"Yes," whispered Leslie.

"I know we haven't really spoken in a while. I don't think it's either of our faults. I want you to know I'm not mad at you, just worried."

Leslie, twirling her hair and rubbing her toes together, made fleeting eye contact with her mother.

"I don't want to make you feel uncomfortable, but I would like to know how you've been doing these past months."

"Fine," Leslie said curtly, twirling her hair more tightly and turning her body away.

Strongly affected by her daughter's remote eye contact, Ceci felt a rush of sadness.

"I miss you, Leslie."

"Whatever," Leslie responded. Even though she appeared annoyed, she was actually happy that her mother had come into her room.

Ceci, however, felt hurt by her daughter's response. She froze. There was not a sound in the room.

Leslie saw her mother's anxious gaze and softened. She had been wanting to talk with her mother, but it had felt like an impossible task to take the first step. Now she felt she had a chance to do so.

"I'm having trouble with my friends," she began.

Ceci sat next to her on the bed. "Is something happening?"

"If I walk in the hall and get a vibe from one of the girls that she doesn't like me, it ruins my whole day."

"What do you mean? Can you tell me more?" said Ceci, hoping Leslie would continue.

"A few months back, all of my friends were going to lots of parties, more than they used to, but I couldn't bring myself to go. I just didn't feel like hanging out. So, eventually, they stopped asking me to be with them."

Ceci remained quiet, waiting for her daughter to continue.

"Mommy, do you think I'm a bad kid? I hate myself. I'm sorry about my room. I just can't bring myself to clean up."

Internally, Ceci was touched when Leslie called her "Mommy," a title she hadn't heard since middle school.

She replied with a sense of urgency. "Sweetie, your room is not important. I'm so sorry I made so much of it. I'll do it with you or for you, or we can leave it this way. Much more important is that you are feeling so bad about yourself. Of course you're not a bad kid! You have no reason to hate yourself. I feel so awful that you've been in so much pain."

"I never told you why I quit dancing." Leslie took a moment and then continued. "I had written to Daddy to come to the show, and he wrote back that he would. But he didn't. I haven't been able to perform since then. It's torn me to pieces. He's always been more tied to his other family. But I held onto the hope that he could be there for me, too. He sent chocolate hearts and an apology that arrived two days after the show, but that only made me mad. I threw them out."

Ceci recognized Leslie's old ability to understand her behavior. This kind of introspection had always helped Leslie cope before. Years of Ceci using her Parental Intelligence had resulted in her daughter having a great deal of self-knowledge. But Ceci was coming to realize that solving problems as deep as this one was a mother-daughter job; Leslie was trying to fly solo, and it wasn't working. Ceci knew that her daughter needed her help to climb out of her despair.

"Oh, sweetheart, I didn't know. It sounds like you really wanted your father to be there to watch you dance."

"Yes, I did. That was when I started to stop talking to you so often. I tried to be my usual self, so it may have been hard to notice, but I was holding so much inside that I began to hide out in my room. I'm sorry. I was worried that if I told you how much I missed him and needed a father now, you would feel you let me down. I know how hard you try to be there for me, even when you punished me for lying about that party."

During some moments when they were both self-absorbed thinking things over, Ceci's mind wandered. She realized again how she had been pushing out Leslie's struggles, keeping them just on the edge of her consciousness in order to keep out memories of her mother's depression. It had taken her much too long to see clearly that her daughter was in such a troubled state of mind. Only with the punishment did her daughter's growing distance hit her so hard. Ceci had acted out of character by using a punishment instead of trying to understand her daughter's mind. It was Leslie's silenced reaction that woke her up to the desperation of her daughter's emotions. Her silence communicated her pain.

Coming back to the present, Ceci realized that even in Leslie's troubled state, when she said she feared she would let her down by being forthcoming about missing her father, Leslie was thinking of her feelings, too. They hadn't been talking during all this time, but they were still connected in each other's minds.

Ceci finally responded to Leslie's comment about lying about the party. Shaking her head, Ceci said, "I don't know what came over me that night. I didn't need to take your phone. You and I should have just talked about what was happening. I really do apologize. I just panicked."

The two sat together quietly for several more moments, and then Ceci continued, "I'm glad we are able to talk together, and I have an idea that might help. Would you like me to talk to your father? It must have been difficult to communicate with him on your own all the time. I know he loves you. He just doesn't know how to show it."

"Yes," responded Leslie, feeling a great release of tension. "I would like you to do that for me."

There was something so caressing in their words as they leaned toward one another, giving Leslie hope.

"I love you, Mommy."

As Ceci hugged her daughter, she felt her love clinging around her again like it had been so many months before. She felt they had returned to their very strong connection. She thought how Leslie's dancing, her painting, her old high spirits, and her present abandoned heart were all her daughter.

Leslie, in return, felt great relief, knowing her mother understood her. She could even tell her about Craig now. She had regained the faithful lifeline that her mother had always represented.

Now that they found each other again, they could continue talking about what both needed. In particular, Ceci felt she could now help her daughter deal with the problem presented by her absent father. Theirs was a unique bond.

Chapter Eleven

A Lonely Place to Call Home

Seventeen-Year-Old Eva

S eventeen-year-old Eva and her parents, Ward and Delle, lived in a modest colonial house in suburban Vineland, New York, about forty minutes from New York City. The houses were surrounded by woods, and neighbors were far apart from each other. The schools were the center of the village, and the children and their education were the focus of these hardworking parents. Eva's parents, however, were not involved in community affairs. They were consumed by their jobs and making ends meet. They set an example of self-discipline and hard work for their daughter.

At five-feet-seven-inches tall, Eva was a svelte seventeen-year-old teenager with auburn hair in her junior year of high school. She was unusually brilliant, sensitive, and kind. She arrived at school on time, did her homework without prompting, and followed the rules. She wanted her parents' approval but struggled between reasoning for herself and blindly abiding by her parents' expectations. This was a tough struggle. Her peers admired her and saw her as a dynamic academic leader. She'd worked all her young life for that image, but she felt something was terribly lacking. With her challenging course load, she sought to create a balance and wanted to develop a social life.

In contrast to her academic success, making friends had never been easy. She had been a loner without best girlfriends or any boyfriends.

Recently, she pulled herself together, pushed past her shyness, and made a few girlfriends who really liked her. One particular week, she was looking forward to a party at a boy's house. It was the first party to which she'd been invited. The host was a popular boy, and her friends would be there. The coveted Friday night arrived, and her curfew was set at midnight. Her father offered to drive Eva and her friends to the party, and a girlfriend's mother had offered to drive them home.

But by 11:30, the girlfriend's mother hadn't arrived. Eva knew she wouldn't meet her curfew. She called her father and bravely told him the whole truth: not only would she be late, but she had also had a beer. She told her father that there was no sense in his coming to get her; it would take half an hour to get to the party, so she'd be late getting home anyway. Finally, the girlfriend's mother arrived at midnight.

Ward, her stern father, met Eva at the door, and told her that no excuses would be accepted. "You know you broke the rules. You're grounded for two weekends. No discussion."

Eva flopped on her bed and thought: *It wasn't my fault. Dad just doesn't get it. He never does. I'm always on time for school, unless the bus is late, but thank goodness Dad doesn't know when that happens, otherwise he'd call the bus company! I tell the truth and get grounded. Last time I do that!*

Ward, who was a quick decision maker, which helped him succeed at work in a financial establishment, applied the same tactics with his daughter. He was very deliberate and purposeful. He thought he was doing the right thing by making sure his daughter knew there were consequences for her actions. However, what Eva took away from his posture was that the next time she did something wrong, she wouldn't be quite so forthcoming.

STEP ONE
Stepping Back

Although Ward believed he had given thought to the punishment, he had only considered seventeen-year-old Eva's action, not his own. He had developed his way of raising Eva all her life, and never questioned the results in a comprehensive way. He didn't step back to take into account her brilliant academic record that developed from her strong self-discipline and good judgment that could be applied to situations outside of school, and he didn't acknowledge that she was also trying to find a way to have a social life. What he did know was that Eva usually met his expectations, and if not, she went along with his punishments. What he didn't know was how Eva felt about the way she was behaving, and how his periodic punishments and her feelings about them were affecting their relationship.

Eva's father's fast reaction to the missed curfew and her drinking beer revealed that he didn't recognize that, as she expanded her social sphere, other people's actions (such as the girlfriend's mother's lateness) would sometimes interfere with his rules. He also didn't consider that some of the experiments Eva might undertake as she was getting older (such as drinking beer) needed to be discussed between them. Without stepping back, such thoughts were not taken into account. He had decided to ground her the moment she called.

As usual, he had left Delle, his wife and Eva's mother, out of his decision-making process to punish Eva. Delle was aware of this decision and complied without considering alternatives. She deferred to her strong, determined husband much in the same way that she kept silent about her frustrations with their marriage. She left disciplining Eva to her husband, but she didn't know that Eva did not respect her for this kind of passivity.

However, something inside Ward was churning. He felt unsettled, restless, not himself. He recalled that when Eva called him, she had warned him she'd be late and had admitted that she'd tried beer.

Then he recalled that when she came home and he grounded her, she had run up to her room in tears, not just placidly following his dictates. He remembered how startled he had been by her unusual reaction. The front hall that had seemed full of life when she went out now seemed dark and empty. *What have I done?* With that thought, he slumped into a well-cushioned chair in the dimly lit living room and fell into deep thought.

This was a defining moment—his restlessness marked the time when Eva's father began to change. He had been emotionally affected by Eva's distressed facial expression and her quick flight up the stairs. His observations shifted his focus from the punishment to feelings inside himself. Eva's reaction had caught him off guard and prompted him to slow down and contemplate his experience.

Because Eva was trying something new—going to a party—Eva's father found his mind wandering to when she was nearly two and tried something new—going down the stairs on her own. She had figured out how to undo the latch on the gate at the top of the stairs and started crawling down the steps backwards. He recalled being scared and not at all impressed, and that he had given Eva the first of what would be many "time-outs." He had reacted as if it were a crisis situation because he had felt a sense of danger. He had acted immediately, put her on a chair upstairs, and made her sit there for five minutes to learn her lesson. He then fixed the gate and told her to not do that again. He later bought a new bolt for the gate.

Eva sat in the chair because even then she was an easy child who listened readily, but Ward wondered, in retrospect, if in fact she had known why she was in the chair. He realized now, for the first time, that she had just made an exciting discovery. Eva's speech was well-developed, and had he taken time to think about what he wanted to accomplish—her safety—he could have put her in the chair but then taken time to sit with her and talk about falling and why the gate was there. He never had these thoughts back then because she was so compliant. Only now, seeing her at seventeen, so upset, did he reconsider that old situation: *Perhaps she wanted me to see her go down the stairs backwards; maybe she expected praise for what she had so cleverly figured out.*

He wondered if he had considered Eva's actions from her two-year-old point of view, if she, too, could have begun to learn about thinking something through. Then as she got older, they could have continued to reason and talk about other risky behavior.

But all of this meant that Ward would have had to pause, step back, and learn more about the positive aspects of his daughter's behaviors when they happened. This would have been a tremendous shift for Eva's father, a shift he wasn't prepared for at that time.

Returning to the present, Ward started to think of many details he had forgotten when he grounded her so abruptly. He recalled how pretty she had looked when she came running down the stairs earlier, thrilled to go out. He thought about her excitedly chatting with her girlfriend in the back seat. He remembered them gaining their composure when they got to the boy's home, and a good-looking fellow greeted them at the door. He had felt proud and was happy for her. Thinking back to her phone call, struggling very hard to suspend his judgment, he was surprised to realize that she had been trying to be honest with him about her new experiences, which was actually something to be pleased about, not to punish automatically. He remembered the sternness he showed when she first got home and how he not only disregarded her feelings, but also forgot all his positive feelings that led up to that moment. He sadly acknowledged that he had lacked empathy. His parenting mindset was changing rapidly because he was stepping back. It was not too late to remedy the situation by understanding it more fully.

STEP TWO
Self-Reflecting

Ward was also his father's first name. They both had red hair, which used to embarrass Eva's father when he was a teen, because he was self-conscious about standing out. He'd begun thinking about his father after the incident with Eva, but he didn't know why. He started searching the web, something that wasn't a common activity for him, but his thoughts about how his father raised him led to a desire to read about new parenting approaches. He knew he was out of the loop of current thinking. He came across an article on Parental Intelligence that stirred him. The idea that his long-forgotten teenage years could be affecting his responses to Eva now struck him hard. His consternation about his reactions to Eva was growing.

Ward and Delle had been distant for many months. Perhaps he should break the ice with her. Maybe if he discussed his decisions about Eva's behavior with his wife, he could begin to understand his patterns of reacting, not only this time, but throughout her preadolescent and adolescent years. He and Delle had known each other since high school. She might be insightful about his behavior.

Delle was quite surprised by her husband's desire to delve into his history. They rarely looked back in time. She saw the intense expression on his face when he came to her, and her coolness toward him began to fall away. She slowly helped him remember that his own father was a harsh disciplinarian. Delle remembered Ward's father as a forbidding man who intimidated her. When they were dating, she didn't like going to his house, and they both remembered the conversations they had back then about her reticence.

It was like a wall came down for Eva's father. He had expected to be a different kind of father for Eva, but his father's ways slipped out. He didn't admit to Delle that he didn't include her in disciplining Eva because he knew she was more flexible and open-minded, which scared him. He hid his feelings by being the authority in the house. He understood that this resembled his parents' approach to parenting him. His mother also took a back seat because his father was so dominating. He told Delle that his father's word was never questioned by his mother and that he had grown up feeling that nearly any rebellion would enrage his father—something he feared.

Experimentation with sex and alcohol was considered immoral in Ward's home. Maybe his father was right, maybe not, but growing up, he had followed blindly and had expected Eva to do the same. He was in his forties now and hadn't yet thought through these questions. He was successful in his career but was rather inept socially. He realized, with his wife's help, that he had to come to his own understanding of these questions so he could believe in the guidance he wanted to give to Eva.

He was taking a big chance by sharing some of these reflections with his wife, but it was a positive step for them as a couple. Delle felt warmer toward Ward than she had in a very long time. They decided they would try to make joint decisions about Eva after discussing situations as they came up.

With these reflections, Ward was able to realize that his reactions went far beyond the instance of breaking the curfew and drinking. He continued to relive how strict his father was about rules of behavior and that he never allowed for any experimentation. He recalled how he felt outside the mainstream of his peers and considered that this had affected how he unwittingly restricted Eva's social life. He had never learned to relate well to other people, so he never knew how to encourage Eva to make more friends. He kept himself in tight control, and throughout his life resisted any temptation to drink more than one glass of wine when out to dinner, and felt guilty doing even that. His father had given him the impression that any drinking at all was irresponsible.

Ward wondered if his father and mother ever had fun. He didn't recall them ever going out and socializing with others, and he realized he and his wife needed to be more outgoing—if they could work out the marital strain that held them back. If they wanted to be able to help Eva, they would have to face their own fears about socializing. He realized further that it was important for Eva to socialize while she was still living at home and could share her experiences with her parents—before she went off to college and had to make decisions on her own. He regretted that he had focused only on her achievements, missing many opportunities to guide her social development. He was now resolute in a new way. He hoped he could remedy this situation with increased empathy for his daughter and her adolescent experiences. He realized that thinking about parenting seemed to bring Delle back to him, too. His world was shifting, and he was shaken but glad.

STEP THREE
Understanding Your Child's Mind

One night, studious Eva forgot to take out the garbage because she was overwhelmed by a great deal of homework. Ward at first believed that she was being rebellious because, when he was Eva's age, he didn't do chores one night to get back at his austere father who screamed at him for the same lapse. He reflexively assumed she was acting out as he had done as a child, and at first, he didn't think to find out what was going on in Eva's mind. But he caught himself this time. He quickly realized he was only focusing on her behavior, not her internal experience. Deeply affected by his discussion with Delle, he asked Eva what was going on. He said she didn't seem herself because she usually would have taken out the garbage by now.

Eva was confused by her father's question. She thought that he was the one who didn't seem like himself. He wasn't yelling at her. She told him she had a lot of homework and was kind of worried about it. She said she really had to go upstairs to get started on it and left hurriedly.

Had Eva's father known how, he could have eased Eva's worry and built upon their relationship. He wasn't ready for that yet, but he was beginning to take into account that her behavior was an expression of something mulling around inside of her.

Unusually pensive, he pondered, *Was the missed chore a sign that might have meaning, not merely careless or defiant behavior?* Ward was beginning to think in this new way, but he needed time to figure out how to have discussions with Eva about her struggles. Ward's Parental Intelligence was growing.

Reflecting again on his childhood years, Ward realized that Eva's missed chore triggered his memory of having been screamed at when he once missed a chore. Understanding that his reaction to Eva's behavior was rooted in his own childhood experience, he was relieved he hadn't ignored Eva's emotional state and punished her the way his father had punished him. He stopped himself from projecting onto Eva his old feelings that not doing chores was a rebellion against him as her father. He could understand that what was on his mind in the past was different from what was on Eva's mind in the present. In the future, he hoped he could find it within himself to open the way for Eva to discuss her anxiety about her perfectionism. He knew she was like that from watching her intensity about her grades and her conscientious approach to her studies at the expense of everything else. Then, in a moment of clarity, he suddenly understood how important the party had been and how insignificant it was that she had been late.

Ward questioned himself: *What was I thinking when I punished her? It wasn't even her fault she was late. She was finally going out with friends, and I found fault with her. And the beer—of course I don't approve of underage drinking, but I should have seen that she was trying to be honest with me. I'm such a fool. How can I remedy my mistake?*

Ward was wondering how to connect with his daughter but did not know how. Learning how to reflect had been an essential step. He had begun to question why that half hour beyond the curfew felt so important to him. He even asked himself why he gave his responsible daughter a curfew at all. He surprised himself with the thought that maybe she could just call during the evening and ask if she could return home at a certain time when she saw how things were going. This might give her the confidence to think for herself, which was more important than his rule. He realized that talking with his wife was rubbing off on him.

He reflected about how his uncompromising father never questioned the impact of his rules on him. He wanted to be different. He was realizing that he had been so out of touch with Eva's mind because he had been so out of touch with what was going on in his own mind.

Ward was awakening to a new way of thinking and feeling. He was coming to terms with the idea that he would have to continue to look inside his heart and mind even further. He thought Delle would continue to help him do this, but turning to her once again with his self-reflections meant looking more deeply into their parental and marital life.

Delle, too, was beginning to come to terms with her passivity. Where did that come from? She had already traced her reticent style back to her teenage years. She had a lot of thinking to do. Meanwhile, she thought self-critically that she was setting a poor example for Eva. She submitted to her husband's actions and never told him how much he upset her. She realized that her lack of interaction with her husband as well as with her daughter left her so out of the emotional sphere of her family that it was as if she led a separate life. They were three people in a house, living together without noticing each had a mind of their own with wishes, desires, and intentions. This was a lonely place to call home.

Each member of the household understood the family's reality through a particular prism. This was evident in both the incident about taking out the garbage and in the incident about the missed curfew. When Ward revealed his new frame of mind by opening up to his wife, she asked him questions about the curfew and chore situations. He told her that Eva responded differently to each. He told Delle about Eva's tight facial expression when he punished her after the party. Her eyes were creased and her lips pursed. But he explained that when he spoke to her more warmly about the chore, pointing out that she didn't seem herself, Eva looked worried but a bit intrigued by his new reaction.

"I'm wondering," he said to Delle, "what she was experiencing each time. Could she have been showing how angry she felt after the party? Was she actually considering talking to me further about her worry over her homework when she skipped her chore?"

While talking with Delle, he began to see things from Eva's perspective. His wife talked compassionately about Eva's perfectionism at school and her need to have a social life. These insights supported his recent thinking and helped him envision making changes in his rules, which might help him get to know his daughter better. Ward's decision to share his view of Eva's behavior with Delle led him to not only find meaning in Eva's behaviors, but also to remember why he loved his wife. He'd hidden from himself how much he missed her. He'd been silencing all of his emotions. How remarkable and enlightening it was to discover how parental and marital relations could be so intertwined.

STEP FOUR
Understanding Your Child's Development

At seventeen, Eva was in late adolescence. At this age, teenagers experience a surge in intellectual development, increasing independence from parents, and a deepening of moral development. It was clear to her parents that Eva's chronological and developmental ages were mixed. Intellectually, they knew she was on the top of her class, evidenced by her brilliant academic achievements. They were proud of the way she showed perseverance, resilience, and a good capacity for handling frustration and disappointment when taking on new challenges. However, while she was responsible and empathic, they were sad to admit they did not have satisfying parent-child relationships. Morally, she appeared compliant with their values, but she needed more time to solidify her own. It took a lot of courage to face that she needed to think more for herself even if that meant disagreeing with them, particularly with her father. They now recognized she fell short in the development of her independence from them and needed support with her social development. She was just beginning to make friends at this late age of seventeen.

Ward and Delle could be quite understanding when they worked together: they understood that friendships would help Eva separate from them emotionally. Friends would not only help her gain some independence from them, but also give her the confidence to leave home to go to college. She needed new experiences to help her form the social skills that would be needed away from home.

When Ward and Delle put the missed curfew and drinking into

perspective, they began to see that this was actually a step forward for Eva. She was asserting her independence and attempting to expand her social spheres. When they realized that missing the curfew was not her fault or a moral transgression, they agreed that a curfew may not even be necessary for Eva at this point; Eva knew this, and for that reason, she wasn't troubled when it was broken. Her father, on the other hand, was now ready to admit that he hadn't comprehended Eva's development by insisting inflexibly on a rule fit for a younger child at an earlier stage of adolescence. In fact, he now thought he needed to foster her social progress by encouraging her to go out more and develop her own rules to live by.

While Ward couldn't condone Eva's drinking, he realized that her honesty on the evening of the party had been an opportunity for a discussion about it, which, unfortunately, he missed. He hoped in the future he would have the wherewithal to talk to Eva about experimenting with social drinking while she was still at home and could talk about it with him. He thought that when she went off to college, if she had no experience, she would find herself at a disadvantage, unprepared for many social situations.

Delle began to think for herself. She realized that she and her daughter needed to work out their relationship so Eva could reconcile her view of her mother before she went out on her own. Delle thought that if Eva could identify with her mother in a positive way, she would be able to accept and enjoy her own femininity and female sexuality. Delle realized that her daughter needed her help and protection. She knew she had to face how important she was for Eva. Her affection and admiration could go a long way in solidifying Eva's self-esteem. Over time, Delle thought she could help her husband continue to refrain from quick reactions and set a different parental tone. She wasn't worried about sex and drugs because she trusted Eva's good judgment.

STEP FIVE
Problem Solving

Delle had begun to change, prompted by Ward's decision to include her more in parenting, which led to her acute observations of Eva's needs. She realized she had been ready to be more of her own person for a long time. She had felt held back, restrained, and frustrated. She realized, although reluctantly at first, that she had hidden resentments toward her husband. At first she was angry he held her back, but then she began to face she was holding herself back. Looking into herself in this way, she was coming to grips with the fact that she was better equipped to face her passivity as a wife and mother than she had previously thought. She was finding a broader, deeper sense of herself, full of emotion and ideas she was getting ready to express. *Thank goodness for Eva's strength,* she thought. *She's leading us both out of from under the shadows.*

One night at dinner, Eva, her mother, and her father were eating silently as usual. This was agitating Eva, and she wondered if, for the first time, she should open Pandora's box and begin to say some things she'd rehearsed in her mind for months. With the curfew issue still on the table and her weekend of punishment coming up, she braced herself and decided it was time to speak. What pushed her forward was her desire to participate in an event with her friends on that weekend.

"Mommy and Daddy, I'm upset that night after night we eat in silence. Now that I've made a few friends and even eaten dinner over at their houses, I've realized that other parents and their teenage daughters are very different than we are. Other families talk at dinner about their days, about fun stuff that happened to them, or about problems they need to solve. We never do that."

Ward and Delle stopped eating at once. Startled, they looked at each other gravely. Although the atmosphere in the room was tense, the minimal light shed by the small chandelier hanging over the table cast a warm glow over the trio.

"Well." Eva's shoulders rose and fell as she spoke. "I'm not following the grounding punishment this weekend. Actually, you can't really make me. I just had this picture in my mind . . . it may be kind of lame, but I thought of Daddy being king, crown and all, carrying me, the princess, up to my room and locking me in there for the weekend and only visiting to give me food and water. But this isn't a fairy tale, and I won't follow the punishment."

Delle found her daughter's dramatic image of her father carrying her to her room somewhat beautiful and tender, although Eva was only consciously aware of the punitive nature of the story. She thought about how much Eva wanted to feel close to her father like his precious little girl, even though she was taking such strides to be grown up. It was this childlike image that moved Delle intensely and prepared her for what was to come.

Eva could feel her knees shaking as she continued. "In fact, on Saturday I've been invited to go to New York City with my friends. We are taking the Long Island Railroad to Penn Station and going to Madison Square Garden for a rock concert. The concert ends at about eleven o'clock and then we'll take the train back. You can't set a curfew because the train schedule determines when I get home. You don't have to drive me to or from the station because other parents have volunteered, and it's all arranged."

Ward was silent. There was so much to absorb. He felt his daughter was being very aggressive, and he'd never seen this side of her. He felt confused and worried. He felt so helpless and powerless—feelings he normally avoided as much as possible. He was an executive in a top position at work and had been the boss at home before his recent discussions with Delle. All at once, he was astounded, remorseful, and proud of Eva for expressing herself.

Given the long silence of both of her parents, Eva felt the courage to continue. "Mommy, I don't think you know me at all. Do you have any idea why I work so hard to take advanced classes in physics, calculus, bio, and chem? It's because I want to be a doctor. It's my junior year, I'm sure you know that," she said somewhat sarcastically, "and all the girls I've been meeting are going with their parents to visit colleges that they will apply to next fall. For months, I've been going online myself researching different pre-med programs."

Eva took a break from speaking to monitor her parents' faces. They seemed intent on listening. She continued, "Neither of you have offered to take me to see any schools. I'll go with my friends and their parents if I have to, but I'd think you'd want to see where I may be living for four years. I know you said you'll pay the tuition, and I plan to work to have money for everything else. I appreciate your generosity and know I am privileged because you both work so hard, but there's a lot more to college than tuition."

Eva was still shaking by then and feeling drained. The silence that had led her to open up more was now bewildering and disorienting. She'd expected her father to blow up at some point and send her to her room. Her mother's silence was less disturbing, because she was always passive, and Eva didn't yet know that her father had begun to include her in their conversations about raising Eva.

Eva almost got up to leave and go lie down when her father finally broke the silence. He knew he had just heard his daughter's hidden voice finally surfacing.

"Eva, the missed curfew really isn't an issue for me anymore, and I take back the punishment."

Eva was astonished. Now it was her time to listen silently.

"I am worried about the trip to the rock concert because you've never even taken a train ride and you haven't had to maneuver through the crowds of young people that will be at Madison Square Garden. At rock concerts, there are a lot of people who may want to sell you drugs, and you'll encounter stoned and drunk kids. I'm also afraid that boys will, well, hit on you. You are very beautiful."

Eva was listening very closely. She didn't know her father even knew about rock concerts, and he'd never said that he thought she was beautiful. She blushed and shivered. Her father had surprised her. What could come next?

"I have an idea," her father went on. "I can see that this trip is very important to you, and at seventeen you should be able to travel on a train with friends without parental supervision. So, today is only Monday, which gives us several days before Saturday. What if I figure out a day I can come home when you get out of school and we can take a trip to Penn Station? I'll show you how to get around and find Madison Square Garden. Then you can try to lead me back to the train. Or we could have dinner first and then go back. I'd feel better knowing you had at least one experience in the city before you go with your friends."

Delle was still quiet but silently overjoyed with her husband's idea. She felt their talking had really made a difference, and he was surprisingly full of ideas for solving what felt like a problem to him. She thought Eva had viewed him as intractable, but now perhaps she could also perceive him as vulnerable and open to her needs.

Eva, recovering from her shock, thought that this was a great idea because she actually was frightened to go, and this way she'd feel more confident and could just enjoy the excitement of Saturday. Her friends didn't have to know she took this practice trip. She felt something she didn't think she had ever felt before. She knew how hard this must be for her father and felt he loved her. She also realized that both she and her father could grow to know each other. There was a potential for them together that she had never envisioned.

"Daddy, thank you so much for thinking about me and how we can work this out, even though you're so worried about it. Truthfully, I'm kind of scared, too, but feel I have a lot of catching up to do socially, so I want to go, even if I'm frightened. Taking a trip with you is a great idea. I can't believe that you're willing to come home from work early and even take me out to dinner alone with you."

She smiled broadly and sighed with relief. "You have another daddy hiding under your crown," she waxed on with a dramatic flair. "Glad to meet you!"

Ward grinned heartily. His daughter was a wonder, and he felt the incredible sensation of being loved by her.

At long last, Delle joined her husband and daughter with a most unexpected emotional response. She started sobbing. Both Ward and Eva stared at her, never having seen her so emotionally uncontained. Eva couldn't hug her, although she thought she should, because she and her mother never showed affection toward each other. Her parents never showed affection in front of her either, so her father just held onto the arms of his chair with his fists. Then, after what felt like forever to Eva, he reached out his hand to his wife.

With that support, she turned to Eva and said, "I am so proud of you."

As Eva started to tear up, Delle said, "I need to wait for another day to talk about colleges, but we are going to plan some trips. Okay, Eva?"

Eva nodded, and looking from her father to her mother, she whispered, "I don't feel like I'm in prison anymore. Thank you both for hearing me out."

Mother, father, and daughter were now able to think about each other's thoughts, feelings, and wishes. They had come an enormous distance from their previously isolated positions. By self-reflecting, Eva's father learned that knowing himself better enhanced his ability to know his daughter. And Eva's mother knew that she and Eva had a chance to find within themselves a chance to become closer during the remainder of her high school career and beyond. It had taken a long time, but they were finally beginning to relate to each other openly. Ward and Delle were unlocking their Parental Intelligence and were deeply grateful to their daughter for lighting the way.

PART THREE

THE FUTURE WITH PARENTAL INTELLIGENCE

Chapter Twelve

The Meeting Ground

When children's voices are heard,
leaders are born.

I created these stories as a way to develop my thinking on Parental Intelligence—first for myself, and now for you. This has been an organic process for me, developing over thirty years of experience with parents and children. As a long-practicing psychoanalyst, I have been able to fundamentally change the way parents and children understand each other, interrelate, and interact. Mapping the relationship between parents and children, I've described how children can be inspirational and influential. Children often challenge their parents' emotional status quo—either directly, through language, or indirectly, through daunting behaviors that can exhaust parents and make them feel helpless until they understand them. Together, these eight stories represent my voice and my role as a social and psychological compass, a mentor to mothers and fathers. The stories reveal unconventional and innovative methods to deepen parents' relationships with infants, children, and adolescents.

In each story, parents and children reached a meeting ground where they saw each other's vantage points and discovered beliefs and values they shared. To get to a place where this meeting of the minds can occur, these mothers and fathers used Parental Intelligence to seek self-understanding by traveling back in time to uncover what predisposed them to reactions that blinded them to their children's intentions. They studied their children's minds and development, getting to know them more comprehensively than they thought possible. As a result, they transformed their original perspectives on problems and uncovered their children's underlying struggles—sometimes slowly, sometimes dramatically. These parents bring rich understandings of their children to the table, and their children are grateful that they can be seen as they really are.

So firmly do I believe in these concepts that I dare claim that if everybody raised children using these ideas, we might very well have a different, better world. Why do I say this?

I received a great deal of support for the answer to this question from my younger millennial son, Rich Hollman, who was raised with Parental Intelligence and has come of age in the twenty-first century. He believes my book comes at a time when, in his words, many people find, "America seems to be in a period of political dogma, a place where certitude is more important than nuance and understanding." This certainty "is masqueraded as strength, but it really comes out of ignorance and fear. I think you can argue that parents fighting with a child, letting their ego get involved, are doing so out of fear of the unknown, unconsciously using a survival reflex, defending themselves unnecessarily. The only thing that can combat fear is knowledge: knowing there's a technique to deal with understanding what's happening in someone else's mind. And that technique is Parental Intelligence. If Parental Intelligence were taught, if people were encouraged to understand one another before reflexively trying to defend themselves, if trying to empathize and know others' minds was seen as a strength, we'd live in a more compassionate, if not more efficient, society."

My son's sentiments seem to be echoed in E. J. Dionne's book, *Our Divided Political Heart: The Battle for the American Idea in an Age of Discontent.* He speaks of the Millennial Generation who are, "at once, more passionately individualistic and more passionately communitarian than any other age group in the country. The Millennials . . . are the most socially tolerant of the generations. They are also the generation most comfortable with racial and ethnic diversity, most open on matters such as gay marriage, and most welcoming to new immigrants . . . such a racially and ethnically diverse generation explains and undergirds many of their attitudes."

So my loving millennial son, raised with Parental Intelligence, is one of many who reflect such feelings about our great nation and are primed to become parents inclined to follow the precepts of Parental Intelligence. It is a good time for the arrival of this book.

The fertility of this approach, however, needs to come early in the lives of our children so that by the time they become our leaders, teachers, engineers, entrepreneurs, musicians, doctors, and parents, self-knowledge and knowledge about the minds of others will be prized. This new generation would recognize that people and situations might not be as they first appear, and they would be open to correcting misconceptions and learning more. Thus, Parental Intelligence offers the building blocks of a civilized and enlightened society.

Here is a common example: As children enter their second and third year, they begin to develop autonomy and individuation. This recurs in adolescence with even more vigor, aided by more developed cognitive abilities. Parents who don't understand these natural strivings often misinterpret their youngsters' voices and actions as oppositionalism. Needless power struggles ensue, and the use of authority may become excessive. In contrast, mothers and fathers with Parental Intelligence understand child development, so they view their children's intentions and motivations to exercise autonomy and individuation in the context of a supportive family, their first community. They support their youngsters' growth with benevolent authority that guides effectively and teaches respect for others.

By the age of four, many children can already recognize that their beliefs do not match reality and accept that reality isn't always as it seems. As parents, we need to cultivate this early discovery. When Parental Intelligence is used early as a way of life, children raised by this type of parenting will be ready to modify their beliefs about others, thereby making problem solving easier and more effective.

What would the future be like if young people learned about Parental Intelligence when they began to consider raising a family? In late adolescence, teenagers are coming to grips with who they are and who they want to become. They often think about raising children. What if these prospective parents were trained in Parental Intelligence so that they could be prepared for what they need to learn to provide a healthy emotional life for their future children?

What would that new generation of parents and their offspring be like? What kinds of families would they be? Children who are raised with Parental Intelligence see problems as opportunities for seeking solutions to difficult predicaments. A generation raised in this way might grow up to be an adult population that thinks through problems by understanding what is going on in other people's minds—that is, other people's intentions, thoughts, beliefs, wishes, desires, motivations, imaginings, and feelings. This would be revolutionary. Complex family compositions would thrive because family members would understand each other. Developing thoughtful interactions by the use of Parental Intelligence might lead to generations of people who would find ways to conduct not only family but national and international affairs through open dialogue rather than by choices that are common now, such as vindication, retaliation, saber rattling, and, ultimately, war.

If Parental Intelligence were commonplace, social understanding would reach new heights. Not only would the needs and desires of others be taken into account, but people would also assess the beliefs others hold about themselves, which would lead to greater understanding of other people's aims. Competition and cooperation would begin to operate differently if people took into account other people's points of view as a matter of course. The intentions of others would be interpreted more accurately.

I believe further that these children would have learned that there are multiple meanings behind behavior that, when recognized and understood, lead to uncovering the essential conflicts that can be resolved with equanimity. For example, challenges we currently face in the United States—individual development in the context of community needs, constitutional debates, civic duty within the framework of market-driven capitalism, the roles of the private and public sectors, and social justice—would still exist, but people raised in the framework of Parental Intelligence would be able to approach these problems without the oversimplification of categorizing people into groups of good or bad, right or wrong, inferior or superior, insider or outsider. Local, national, and international challenges other countries face, which are beyond the scope of this book, would be understood by children raised with Parental Intelligence, who become adults able to tackle their nations' problems because they recognize the deep complexities involved.

I do not mean to suggest that all children raised with Parental Intelligence would think alike; quite the contrary. But I know they would all think, reason, and question while searching for truths from various perspectives. One of the things that makes humans different from all other species is the ability to know and understand their own minds and the minds of others. Parental Intelligence exemplifies and exercises this capacity.

My attempt to flesh out Parental Intelligence has been a challenging task. Through this process, I have come to believe that a future with this kind of intelligence would be a hopeful one. The social and political role of parents in society would be enhanced as they advance new generations of masterful communicators.

In a world of uncertainties, these parents and their children could become experts at monitoring their own and other people's social expressions and behaviors, which could foster knowledgeable engagement and further peaceful diplomacy. Their exquisite grasp of the intentions, motives, feelings, and actions of others would serve those disposed to become leaders in their communities and the world at large. Their expertise in conceptualizing how they and others perceive and think about the world could give them the skills to bridge divides among diverse social groups. The children, who have managed to operate successfully in the intimate, social world of complex family relationships by using reasoning and reflective exchanges during emotionally laden conflicts, could transpose these abilities to larger and larger contexts. Research on these possibilities remains to be done, but it is certainly conceivable that sophisticated social understanding on a small scale could eventually progress exponentially to reshape relations on a broad, far encompassing scale. The window is wide open.

References

Bretherton, Inge. 2009. "Intentional Communication and the Development of an Understanding of Mind." *In Children's Theories of Mind: Mental States and Social Understanding*, edited by D. Frye and C. Moore, 49–76. New York: Psychology Press.

Cohan, Carolyn Pape, and Philip A. Cohan. 2000. *When Partners Become Parents: The Big Life Change for Couples.* London: Lawrence Erlbaum Associates Publishers.

Condon, W. S. 1979. "Neonatal Entrainment and Enculturation." *Before Speech: The Beginnings of Interpersonal Communication*, edited by Margaret Bullowa, 131–48. Cambridge, UK: Cambridge University Press.

Cutler, Eustacia. 2004. *A Thorn in My Pocket: Temple Grandin's Mother Tells the Family Story.* Arlington, Texas: Future Horizons, Inc.

Dionne, E. J. 2012. *Our Divided Political Heart: The Battle for the American Idea in an Age of Discontent.* New York: Bloomsbury.

Ekman, Paul. 2007. *Emotions Revealed: Recognizing Faces and Feelings to Improve Communication and Emotional Life.* New York, New York: Henry Holt and Co., LLC.

Grandin, Temple, and Sean Barron. 2005. *Unwritten Rules of Social Relationships.* Arlington, Texas: Future Horizons, Inc.

Hollman, Rich (March 30, 2014). Email correspondence on American politics and Parental Intelligence.

Lamb, Michael E., ed. 2010. *The Role of the Father in Child Development.* Canada: John Wiley and Sons.

Meins, Elizabeth, Charles Fernyhough, Emma Fradley, and Michelle Tuckey. 2001. "Rethinking Maternal Sensitivity: Mothers' Comments on Infants' Mental Processes Predict Security of Attachment at 12 Months." *Journal of Child Psychology and Psychiatry.* 42 (5): 637–48.

Paul, Annie Murphy. 2010. *Origins: How the Nine Months Before Birth Shape the Rest of Our Lives.* New York: Free Press.

Livingston, Gretchen 2014. "Growing Number of Dads Home with the Kids." Pew Research Social and Demographic Trends. June 5, 2014 http://www.pewsocialtrends.org/2014/06/05/growing-number-of-dads-home-with-the-kids.

Pruett Kyle. 2000. *Fatherneed: Why Father Care is as Essential as Mother Care for Your Child.* New York: Broadway Press.

Pruett, Kyle, and Marsha Pruett. 2009. *Partnership Parenting: How Men and Women Parent Differently—Why It Helps Your Kids and Can Strengthen Your Marriage.* Cambridge, Massachusetts: Life Long.

Raeburn, Paul. 2014. *Do Fathers Matter? What Science Is Telling Us About the Parent We've Overlooked.* New York: Scientific American/Farrar, Straus, and Giroux.

Szejer, Myriam. 2005. *Talking to Babies: Healing with Words on a Maternity Ward.* Boston: Beacon Press Books.

Trevarthen, Colwyn. 1979. "Communication and Cooperation in Early Infancy: A Description of Primary Intersubjectivity." *Before Speech: The Beginnings of Interpersonal Communication*, edited by Margaret Bullowa, 321–48. Cambridge, UK: Cambridge University Press.

Walsh, Carolyn J., Anne E. Storey, Roma L. Quinton, and Katherine E. Wynne-Edwards. 2000. "Hormonal Correlates of Paternal

Responsiveness in New and Expectant Fathers." *Evolution and Human Behavior* 21 (2): 79–95.

Winnicott, Donald W. (1958) *Through Pediatrics to Psycho-Analysis: Collected Papers*. New York: Basic Books.

Wynne-Edwards, Katherine E. 2004. "Why Do Some Men Experience Pregnancy Symptoms such as Vomiting and Nausea When Their Wives are Pregnant?" *Scientific American*. June 28, 2004. www.scientificamerican.com/article.cfm?id=why-do-some-men-experienc.

Index

About the Author

LAURIE HOLLMAN, PhD, is a psychoanalyst with specialized clinical training in infant-parent, child, adolescent, and adult psychotherapy covering the life-span.

Dr. Hollman has been on the faculties of New York University, The Society for Psychoanalytic Study and Research, Long Island University, and The Long Island Institute for Psychoanalysis.

She has written extensively for various publications on infant, child, and adolescent development including the *Psychoanalytic Study of the Child*, *The International Journal of Infant Observation*, and *The Inner World of the Mother*. She has also written on subjects relevant to parents of divorce for the *Family Law Review*, a publication of the New York Bar Association. As a columnist for *Newsday's Parents & Children Magazine* and the *Long Island Parent* for almost a decade, she has written numerous articles on parenting.

Dr. Hollman writes the "Parental Intelligence" column for *Moms Magazine* and blogs for *Huffington Post*. She is also a feature writer for *The Bloggy Moms Network* and a guest writer for popular parenting websites including *Natural Parenting Network*, *Positive Parenting Ally*, *Our Parenting Spot*, and *Parenting London Child*.

About Familius

Welcome to a place where parents are celebrated, not compared. Where heart is at the center of our families, and family at the center of our homes. Where boo-boos are still kissed, cake beaters are still licked, and mistakes are still okay. Welcome to a place where books—and family—are beautiful. Familius: a book publisher dedicated to helping families be happy.

Visit Our Website: www.familius.com

Our website is a different kind of place. Get inspired, read articles, discover books, watch videos, connect with our family experts, download books and apps and audiobooks, and along the way, discover how values and happy family life go together.

Join Our Family

There are lots of ways to connect with us! Subscribe to our newsletters at www.familius.com to receive uplifting daily inspiration, essays from our Pater Familius, a free ebook every month, and the first word on special discounts and Familius news.

Become an Expert

Familius authors and other established writers interested in helping families be happy are invited to join our family and contribute online content. If you have something important to say on the family, join our expert community by applying at:

www.familius.com/apply-to-become-a-familius-expert

Get Bulk Discounts

If you feel a few friends and family might benefit from what you've read, let us know and we'll be happy to provide you with quantity discounts. Simply email us at specialorders@familius.com.

Website: www.familius.com

Facebook: www.facebook.com/paterfamilius

Twitter: @familiustalk, @paterfamilius1

Pinterest: www.pinterest.com/familius

The most important work you

ever do will be within the walls

of your own home.

CPSIA information can be obtained
at www.ICGtesting.com
Printed in the USA
FSOW02n0407081015
966FS

9 781942 934042